EVERY-PER

EVERY-PERSON MINISTRY

Reaching out in Christ

Teresa Morgan

First published in Great Britain in 2011

Society for Promoting Christian Knowledge
36 Causton Street
London SW1P 4ST
www.spckpublishing.co.uk

Copyright © Teresa Morgan 2011

The author and publisher have made every effort to ensure that the external website and
email addresses included in this book are correct and up to date at the time
of going to press. The author and publisher are not responsible for
the content, quality or continuing accessibility of the sites.

Unless otherwise noted, Scripture quotations are taken from the New Revised Standard
Version of the Bible, Anglicized Edition, copyright © 1989, 1995 by the Division
of Christian Education of the National Council of the Churches
of Christ in the USA. Used by permission. All rights reserved.
One extract is from the Authorized Version of the Bible (The King James Bible),
the rights in which are vested in the Crown, and is reproduced by permission
of the Crown's Patentee, Cambridge University Press.

The publisher and author acknowledge with thanks permission to reproduce extracts
from the following. Every effort has been made to seek permission to
use copyright material reproduced in this book. The publisher apologizes
for those cases where permission might not have been sought and,
if notified, will formally seek permission at the earliest opportunity.
'The African Creed' from *Christianity Rediscovered* by V. Donovan is © SCM Press,
2001 and is reproduced by permission of Hymns Ancient & Modern Ltd;
copyright © Orbis Books, 2003.
The Lausanne Covenant is © 1974, The Lausanne Movement.
'Though he was divine' and 'We believe in God the Father': Words:
Michael Perry © Mrs B Perry
Administered by The Jubilate Group,
4 Thorne Park Road, Torquay TQ2 6RX, UK
copyrightmanager@jubilate.co.uk
USED BY PERMISSION

British Library Cataloguing-in-Publication Data
A catalogue record for this book is available from the British Library

ISBN 978–0–281–06447–2
eBook ISBN 978–0–281–06623–0

Typeset by Graphicraft Ltd, Hong Kong
Manufacture managed by Jellyfish
First printed in Great Britain by CPI
Subsequently digitally printed in Great Britain

Produced on paper from sustainable forests

To Catharine, with love and thanks

Contents

————•◆•————

Contents

Preface

Warm thanks, as always, are due to the congregations of St Mary and St Nicholas, Littlemore, and St Andrew, Sandford-on-Thames, who were the first to try out the material on which this book is based. I am grateful to Vivien Foster, Catharine Morgan, Robert Morgan, Prue Sykes and Claire Wigg, who each read the manuscript in draft and made many helpful comments and suggestions.

Introduction:
ministry for all believers

This is a book about Christian ministry: the ministry which every Christian has in all the places where we live and work. It grew out of the conviction that every Christian *has* a ministry. Everyone can help to make the love of God visible and tangible. Everyone is called to be Christ's hands and feet on earth.

The themes which are explored here began life as a parish course, which ran jointly one summer in two neighbouring parishes, Sandford-on-Thames and Littlemore, on the edge of Oxford. We had just completed our annual journey from Advent to Pentecost, and were thinking that it was a pity there was no Pentecost season – as there is, for instance, in The Episcopal Church in the USA – to give us more time to reflect on this new phase of God's work on earth. We wanted to go on following the story of Jesus' disciples, whose lives had been so dramatically changed by their encounter with Christ and the gift of the Holy Spirit.

At Pentecost, we had celebrated the moment when Jesus' disciples became fully fledged apostles. From being people who had learned to see God in Christ, they became people in whom others saw and heard Christ. Inspired by the Holy Spirit, they became people through whom the Spirit acted in the world. By putting their lives in God's hands, they evolved from followers of doubtful reliability into prophets, teachers, healers and leaders – people with a mission and a ministry.

Our own encounter with Christ had changed our lives too. We were keen to explore what Pentecost could do with us.

We realized, of course, that there is more to the making of apostles than the miracle at Pentecost. Matthew, Mark and Luke all describe Jesus' disciples as apostles even during Jesus' lifetime.[1]

1

Later in the Acts of the Apostles, some people – notably Paul – are called apostles who did not know Jesus in his lifetime and were not among the disciples at Pentecost.[2] Becoming an apostle is a process of development as well as a moment of transformation, and many people have followed in the disciples' footsteps since that first Pentecost. But everyone who is called an apostle in the New Testament has one thing in common: they have been commissioned – sent out – to minister in Jesus' name.

The word 'apostle' means 'one who is sent', from the Greek *apostello*, 'I send' or 'I send out'. 'Jesus summoned his twelve disciples,' says Matthew (10.1), 'and gave them authority over unclean spirits, to cast them out, and to cure every disease and every sickness.' He sent them (*apesteilen*) all over Israel, to heal the sick, raise the dead, exorcise demons and proclaim the good news that the kingdom of heaven has come near. 'See,' says Jesus, 'I am sending you out (*apostello*) like sheep into the midst of wolves; so be wise as serpents and innocent as doves.'[3]

The group which met that summer at Littlemore decided to explore where God might be sending us. We didn't see ourselves as heroic figures of faith, like the first apostles – not at all. But as followers of Christ we were used to the idea that we were following in the footsteps of the disciples. We had sung the Pentecost hymns: 'Breathe on me, breath of God'; 'Come, Holy Ghost, our souls inspire'; 'Forth in your name, O Lord, I go'. It was hard not to believe that at Pentecost we were being invited to follow the first disciples into apostleship – into ministry.

Several of us were already healers, teachers and leaders of one kind or another. Di had been a nurse, and Ray was a member of the St John Ambulance Brigade. Julian taught in a school, Judy in a prison. Jean helped in the local primary school, and Mo helped to run tea dances for the elderly. Through institutions from the credit union to the Women's Institute, and through our two churches, the group between them did a great deal in the community.

We all saw our various jobs and activities as in some way expressions of our faith. What we did, we did as Christians, if not because we were Christians. But we wanted to go further. Might there be other ministries waiting for us?

The simplest and greatest ministry, which Jesus gives to all his followers, is, 'Love God and love your neighbour.'[4] Jesus also several times invites his followers to share their material and spiritual wealth with people who have less. 'Let your light shine before others, so that they may see your good works and give glory to your Father in heaven.' '[G]o, sell what you own, and give the money to the poor, and you will have treasure in heaven; then come, follow me.'[5] St Paul, in one of the group's favourite passages, describes the 'fruit of the Spirit' as 'love, joy, peace, patience, kindness, generosity, faithfulness, gentleness, and self-control.'[6]

In every generation, a small number of exceptional Christians have taken literally Jesus' exhortation to sell everything they owned to follow him. But most of us have aspired to love God and our neighbours while living among them – creating a home, bringing up a family, holding down a job. It was in this kind of ordinary life that the members of the discussion group believed their ministries might lie. Between us, we lived, worked and socialized in many different contexts, with many different people. We should, we felt, be in a good position to practise loving our neighbours and sharing the fruit of the Spirit quite widely.

Gradually, we came to focus on five forms of ministry which we could all practise in and through our different occupations: love, listening, prophecy, reconciliation and teaching. We also identified two things which might help us to minister better: dismantling the unhelpful passions in ourselves which stop us attending to others, and praying in ways which we could carry with us in our daily lives. These seven topics became the seven chapters of this book.

Priesthood for all believers

The absence of a Pentecost season in our church calendar was not the only inspiration for the Pentecost discussion group. It also grew out of my own experience over several years of being a 'minister in secular employment' or 'worker priest'.

When I first felt called to ordination, I was working as a university lecturer. Without really knowing why, I felt strongly that I should stay in post. In due course, I was ordained and began to work part-time and unpaid in a parish while continuing to teach. Over the next few years, I thought a good deal about what it meant to be a priest working full-time in a secular job.

Priesthood has many dimensions, from the practical business of looking after church buildings to the mystical role of representing Christ at the Eucharist. Priests are called to be prophets, speaking out against injustice and inhumanity in the world around them, and pastors, caring for people in good times and bad. They study and teach Scripture and tradition. They pray for those around them. When they administer the sacraments they act as a medium of divine forgiveness and blessing. Above all, they give themselves heart, mind, soul and strength to God, and try to live in such a way as to express and communicate God's love for the world, and the opportunity which is given to us all to accept and be transformed by that love.

I didn't see myself as a priest in my parish and a lecturer at work, but as living one life of faith in several places. Bit by bit, a few ideas began to germinate about how someone might be a priest in and for their working community.

It would not involve talking about religion very much, unless other people wanted to. Most of my colleagues were not religious, or were religious but not Christian. I respected them personally; I respected their religious and other commitments; I did not plan to give them indigestion by telling them over lunch what I thought they ought to believe. It seemed to me that ministering at work should be more about 'showing' than 'telling'.

Day by day, I would try to be attentive to the people around me, especially if they were in need of practical help, encouragement or just a listening ear. I would speak out and act, if necessary, against inequality, unkindness or injustice. I would try to live in harmony with my colleagues and students, and to foster forgiveness and

4

reconciliation whenever we fell out. I would look for ways of teaching, writing, taking part in meetings or doing routine administration that made my institution a more loving, peaceful, joyful place, and helped it share those qualities with the wider world. Finally, I would say every day to God, 'Not my will but yours be done', and wait and see what God did with my obedience.

No sooner had I worked out this scheme than it became obvious that there was nothing especially priestly about it. *All* Christians are called to love one another, to look after one another, to live in peace, to defend the oppressed, to live their faith every day and to do God's will. To live and work as I hoped to do, I realized, I hadn't needed to get ordained at all.

What's more, my own Church had been telling me so for 500 years.

The 'priesthood of all believers' is an idea shared, in one form or another, by all Reformed or Protestant Churches. It affirms that God speaks directly to, and works directly through, all people of faith. It was developed out of a reading of 1 Corinthians 12 by Martin Luther (1483–1546), who spent his early adulthood as a Catholic monk.

Catholic orthodoxy taught the young Luther that he would come to salvation through the institutions and sacraments of the Church – above all, through baptism, absolution and the Eucharist. These sacraments could only be administered by priests, who acted as intermediaries – 'carriers' – of God's grace and love. But however hard he tried, Luther could not feel that the rituals he took part in every day, and the sacraments he received, brought him into the presence of a forgiving God. Then one day, alone in his cell, he had the overwhelming experience that he *was* forgiven. This experience, together with his study of the New Testament, convinced him that salvation is a gift from God directly to each person who has faith. There is no need of any intermediary.

That is not to say that human beings can't embody and express the love of God, and move others to faith by their own faith and love. On the contrary, Luther says, *everyone* can do that, and should.

In this sense, all believers are priests: we can all help each other to experience God's grace and love.[7]

Luther's ideas were taken further by other reformers, including, in England, Archbishop Thomas Cranmer (1489–1556). Cranmer, too, believed that God offers love and forgiveness directly to all human beings. People respond by putting their faith in God, who 'justifies' us: brings us back into our right relationship of love and trust with Godself. All people of faith can help to bring the love of God to the rest of the world by the way they live and speak. As the Methodist Church would later put it: 'The ideal church does not consist of an active few – the ordained clergy – and the passive many, the laity who are just content to be recipients of benefits from their clergy; all are called to *serve* the Church of Christ.'[8]

Not everyone is comfortable with the phrase 'the priesthood of all believers', and these days it is not much used in most Churches. The point it makes, however, is an important one: we are all ministers, and we can all embody and express the love of God by the way we live, and move other people to faith by the way we speak and act.

Apostles and role models

The members of the Pentecost discussion group found the idea of the priesthood of all believers interesting, but were more inspired by the example of the apostles. The apostles, they felt, were particularly good role models for later Christians.

For a start, they came from very varied backgrounds. Some (like Matthew the tax collector) were probably comfortably off; others (like the fishermen James and John) may have been relatively poor. Most will have spoken Aramaic, but some (like Philip and Andrew, who have Greek names) probably spoke Greek too. Most were born in Israel, but Paul came from Tarsus in modern southern Turkey.

When Jesus called his soon-to-be disciples, there probably wasn't much to distinguish them from any other working men of Galilee.

Most of them are likely to have been no more than ordinarily religious.[9] Following Jesus, however, developed in them a profound trust in God, unquenchable confidence, high hope and unshakeable faithfulness. They became an inspiration for many of the people they met.

The apostles are described as having diverse qualities and abilities. Some were known mainly as teachers, others as healers too; some were natural leaders and others followers. Some worked alone and others in a team. They exercised their ministries in different ways. Some (like James the brother of Jesus) seem never to have moved far from home, while others (like Peter and, according to tradition, Thomas) travelled halfway across the known world. Some were supported financially in their ministry by other Christians, while others (like Paul who, according to Acts, made tents) supported themselves. Between them, they show us something of the infinitely many ways in which Christian lives can be given to God.

Most of their ministries lay outside formal religious institutions. In the early years, the apostles are shown trying to proclaim the good news in synagogues and in the precincts of the Jerusalem Temple. They are generally thrown out, because their proclamation that Jesus is the Messiah is unacceptable to most Jewish leaders. It was out of the question for them to attach themselves to pagan temples, so they took their ministry into private houses and public spaces: roads and ships, prisons and theatres, law courts and marketplaces.

If this development was largely accidental, it was also wonderfully appropriate. The life and teaching of Jesus had challenged many of the religious and social boundaries with which his followers had grown up: boundaries between different groups of Jews, Jews and Samaritans, Jews and gentiles, clean and unclean, men and women, powerful and powerless. After Jesus' death, his followers increasingly came to see the gospel as good news for *all* people. Christ was the light of the whole world, and it was right and proper that his message should be heard, his love experienced, everywhere and by everyone.

Jesus taught his disciples to give themselves, heart, soul, mind and strength, to God and to their neighbours – and they did. As a result, people were drawn to them and inspired by them almost as they had been by Jesus himself. In their understanding of mission as something which happened anywhere and everywhere; in their willingness to step over traditional boundaries; in the variety of their gifts and ministries; in their capacity to change and grow in response to Christ's call; above all, in their dedication of every aspect of their lives to the service of God, the Pentecost discussion group felt that the first apostles were an inspiration and an example to us today.

Ministry today

Each of the following chapters explores one way in which Christians today can follow the example of the apostles and minister in all the places where we live and work. They are arranged in what is intended to be a helpful order, but they can be read in any sequence.

Most people find that some aspects of ministry come more easily to them than others. This is only natural: as Paul says, there are varieties of gifts from the same Spirit.[10] Often, however, we find where our main ministry lies by exploring a range of possibilities. And all the forms of ministry discussed here are close to the heart of apostolic life, so all of them are worth consideration.

The foundation of all our activities as Christians is love. God's love for the world reaches out to us through Jesus Christ and the Holy Spirit. Through our love for God and Christ we are reconciled with God, and Jesus repeatedly teaches us to love God and one another. We therefore begin by exploring the nature of Christian love, who we are called to love, and how.

One of the most important aspects of love is attentiveness to others – who they are, what they say and do, and what they need from us. Thinking about love therefore leads us to the practice of listening. Being attentive to people and to the world around us often brings problems into focus, so from listening we move on to prophecy. Prophecy challenges individuals and societies to face their problems and address them, which can be traumatic and divisive, so Chapter 4 focuses on peacemaking and reconciliation: how to preserve or restore harmony in disrupted families and communities.

Every life of ministry develops alongside our own spiritual development and is supported by it. If we want to minister effectively, we need to be aware of the problems within ourselves which stop the Spirit acting freely through us, and to practise defusing them. At the same time, it is important to practise attending to God, living consciously in God's presence, constantly as we go about all our other business. Chapters 5 and 6 explore some ways of doing both these things.

Last but not least, we come to the way we express our faith verbally and talk to others about it. This chapter is placed last because, although we want to be ready to talk about our faith, it isn't easy to do and not everyone wants to listen. Actions speak louder than words, and a life of integrity which is devoted heart, soul, mind and strength to God, speaks loudest of all.

Each chapter is designed both to be readable in itself, and to be usable as a basis for discussion. At the end of each chapter there are some questions for discussion, and at the very end there are suggestions for further reading and other resources.

1

The meanings of love

If one word can sum up the relationship between God and humanity, it must be love. Love is the foundation on which all our relationships are built: the love of God which embraces us; the love of Christ, which awakens us to God's love and teaches us how to respond; and our own love, which joins God in mending our strained and spoiled relationships. So it seemed obvious to the Pentecost discussion group that the place we should start thinking about our ministry was with love.

Some of the best-loved passages of the Bible tell us to love God and love our neighbours, and some of the best-known verses about love, put side by side, sum up the good news of Jesus Christ for many people. 'God so loved the world that he gave his only Son, so that everyone who believes in him may not perish but may have eternal life' (John 3.16). 'If you love me, you will keep my commandments' (John 14.15). 'This is my commandment, that you love one another as I have loved you. No one has greater love than this, to lay down one's life for one's friends' (John 15.12–13). 'God is love, and those who abide in love abide in God, and God abides in them' (1 John 4.16).

But love is an elastic word, with different meanings in different contexts. If we want to practise it as part of our life of ministry, we need some sense of its particular meaning for Christians. What's more, Christians have held different views about who we should love. We in the Pentecost group therefore asked ourselves three questions: What is love? Who should we love? And how should we love? We began by reflecting on the meaning of the word which early Christians used for love.

What is love?

The earliest Christian word for love is the Greek *agape*. *agape* was a fairly rare word before Christians adopted it, which may be one reason why they did. There were several other words in wider use: *eros* (erotic love), *philia* (family affection, friendship or alliance), and *storge*, which overlaps with both the others.[1]

Though *agape* was rare, there is a verb, *agapan*, which was quite common. *agapan* means 'to be pleased' or 'to be contented', to love someone like a member of the family or to be a good neighbour. It is also the word used in the Septuagint (the ancient Greek translation of the Hebrew Bible) for the love between God and humanity.[2] When Moses, for example, proclaims in the book of Deuteronomy (6.4–5), 'Hear, O Israel: the LORD is our God, the LORD alone. You shall love the LORD your God with all your heart, and with all your soul, and with all your might', the word for 'love' is *agapan*.

It seems likely that the writers of the New Testament, who knew the Septuagint well, intended Christian *agape* to echo the meanings of *agape* and *agapan* in the Septuagint. Christian love was therefore the kind of love which God offers to human beings and human beings offer to God, and to one another through God's grace. It is the kind of love which exists between members of a family or between neighbours.

The only passage in the New Testament which tries to describe love at length is 1 Corinthians 13.4–7. This chapter is often read in a modern translation such as the NRSV, which begins, 'Love is patient; love is kind; love is not envious or boastful or arrogant or rude . . .' This doesn't quite do justice to St Paul, because Paul doesn't say that love *is* various things. Paul says that love *does* things: 'Love suffers long, and does good; love does not envy; love does not boast or puff itself up; it does not disgrace itself; it does not seek its own advantage; it does not stir up trouble; it does not speak evil; it does not rejoice in injustice, but rejoices with what is good. It bears everything, believes everything, hopes everything, endures everything.'[3]

Paul's list is a practical one, and it comes down to three kinds of action. Love does good. It lives in harmony with people. And it never stops believing in and hoping for good.

For the writers of the New Testament, as for us, love was an emotion which produces feelings. But although 1 Corinthians 13 shows that Paul wants our faith to involve feelings, thoughts, words and actions, Paul is not particularly interested in exploring how love makes us feel. The same is true of St John's Gospel, in Jesus' great sermon on love (13.34–35, 14.15–24, 15.9–17). Jesus tells his followers to love one another as he has loved them – and his examples of love are of actions rather than feelings.

In modern Western culture, we are intensely interested in feelings. We invest a huge amount of time, energy and money investigating and talking about our own feelings and other people's. When we fall in or out of love, or we are involved in any kind of loving relationship, it is often how it makes us feel that interests us most. Early Christians seem to have been more interested in how love makes us act, and the effect of our love on other people. It is important to them that emotion and action go together, but the significance of *agape* lies not so much in how it feels as what it does.

What, then, the Pentecost group asked itself, does family or neighbourly love do that makes it such a good model for Christians?

Family love and neighbourly love

Perhaps the first thing it does is simply to recognize and accept that other people are there.

Virtually all of us live, all the time, surrounded by other people, all of whom have exactly as much right to be in the world as we do ourselves. This is true even if we live alone – even if we live as a hermit at the top of a mountain. For most of us it is true in very obvious ways: we share our homes, the bus queue, the local shops, the office, the rush-hour traffic.

Most of us don't choose the people we live and work among,

or if we do, we choose them once for years to come. Some of our relationships last a lifetime. So unless we're going to try to cut ourselves off from the whole world around us, we have to accept that our family and our neighbours are part of our lives. That means that unless we're going to spend our whole lives falling out and fighting, we have to learn to get along. In the process of getting along, we gradually learn to understand one another.

I remember the day when I came home from school and announced that I hated my teacher. I was six. 'She shouts all the time! She made us keep our heads on the table *all afternoon* and we hadn't done *anything wrong!*' 'Hmm,' said my mother, 'I think she's having a difficult time.' The teacher was, I learned much later, looking after a seriously ill husband at home. But that day, I was baffled and indignant. Teachers were teachers. You did what they told you but you didn't have to understand them.

As I grew up, I was often struck by how tolerant my parents and other adults were, even of quite annoying or difficult people – and the longer they had known them, the more tolerant they seemed to be. Once, I pointed out to my college tutor all the defects of a well-known author I'd been reading. 'He was a colleague of my father's', my tutor mused. 'He was badly injured in the Second World War.' Since I was no longer six but 20, her words stopped me in my tracks. I went away and pondered them for a long time.

Nowadays, when I'm talking to children or to my own students, I often catch myself sounding like my parents and tutors. I have known my friends and colleagues for 20 years or more, shared some of their experiences and seen them grow up. Because I know a bit about why they are the way they are, it is easier to accept their strengths and weaknesses and eccentricities, as I hope they accept mine.

As we grow older, we also begin to appreciate how the people around us have affected us – the way we think and behave – and how we have affected them. One of my friends credits the vicar who trained her as a curate with curing her (more or less) of perfectionism. 'If a thing's worth doing,' he would say, 'it's worth doing badly. The important thing is to do something and get people to join in.' This motto was good for every aspect of parish life, and ten years later, she says, she's still learning how true it is.

The longer we know one another, the more closely our lives become intertwined. And the better we know one another, the more obvious it becomes that although we are all different, we are all also, in some ways, very much alike.

We all need to give love and receive it. We all have hopes and dreams. We all make mistakes, and hurt other people, and get hurt ourselves. We all change, and learn to live with change, and most of us find ourselves, at some point in our lives, doing or experiencing something we never expected to do or experience. There are things about ourselves that each of us wishes were different, but we all hope for happiness and fulfilment.

At least – as some of the discussion group pointed out – all this is true in theory. In practice, most of us divide our families and neighbours into the ones we like and spend time with, and the ones we don't, and the second group get rather less tolerance and understanding than the first.

What is more, the richer and more materially secure we are, the more choosy we tend to become. In particular, we tend to know our neighbours less well. In many an affluent suburb, a 'good neighbour' becomes not someone we share our lives with, but someone who keeps themselves to themselves, and doesn't bother us with their noise or badly bagged rubbish.

We can guess that the same was often true in the world of the New Testament. Despite the fact that 'Love God and love your neighbour' had summed up the Jewish Law for centuries, the Gospels show Jesus having to remind people of it regularly. His parables are full of foolish or wicked individuals who try to keep their wealth to themselves or increase it at other people's expense. The parable of the Good Samaritan is told to answer the question, 'Who is my neighbour?' and to show that our neighbours include people we thought were nothing to do with us.

The experience of Jesus and his followers was not, though, only one of wealth and unneighbourliness. In first-century Israel, a large proportion of the population lived close to the breadline, in a state with virtually no welfare provision. Jesus lived and worked among people – fishermen, craftsmen, small farmers – many of whom will have been very poor. In such communities, neighbours are not just the people next door: they are each other's life support system. They're more likely to help one another because they know at first hand how quickly and irremediably poverty can collapse into destitution, sickness and death. It is surely out of his experience of such communities that Jesus tells his followers to love their neighbours, and love one another like neighbours.

My neighbour, myself

Even when we're not immediately dependent on our neighbours for food or shelter, nearly all of us accept that we are dependent on some people for some things. The challenge for most of us is to recognize just how far this dependence goes: how many people we depend on, and how fundamentally our interdependence shapes our lives.

'No man is an island', wrote the seventeenth-century poet and clergyman John Donne.

> No man is an Island, entire of it self; every man is a piece of the Continent, a part of the main; if a clod be washed away by the sea, Europe is the less, as well as if a promontory were, as well as if a manor of thy friends or of thine own were; any man's death diminishes me, because I am involved in Mankind; And therefore never send to know for whom the bell tolls; it tolls for thee.[4]

What Donne sees so clearly, and what most of us so often forget, is that as human beings we are *all* related and *all* dependent on one another. We are one species, descended biologically from the same few ancestors. We live on one planet, whose resources we share. We belong to economies, societies and cultures which are interconnected in millions of ways. In the twenty-first century, we can go even further than Donne, and recognize that our species is part of a much greater web of interrelated beings. We belong to an infinite continuum of ever-evolving life. We are literally one materiality; one creation; one body.

And the way we develop as parts of this body is to a great extent the way we are shaped by others – by our genes, upbringing and environment, by what happens to us and the people we share our lives with. In all our uniqueness, we all help to form one another: physically, mentally, spiritually and emotionally.

It follows that the way other people develop is just as important to us as the way we develop ourselves. If we want to be healthy and happy, loved and fulfilled, we must want the same for others, because our lives depend on the lives around us.

When we recognize this, it changes all our relationships. It becomes obvious that we need to look after each other as carefully as we would like to be looked after, or as we would look after ourselves. We must love our neighbours as ourselves, and treat them as we hope they'll treat us, because if anyone is to flourish in the world, everyone must be helped to flourish. The way we love one another is, in fact, the way we love ourselves.

And the way we love ourselves is the way we love God, in whom all creation lives and moves and has its being. No one captures this better than Teilhard de Chardin (1881–1955), a French priest, scientist and theologian who wrote extensively on the unity of creation and its relationship with the divine. He saw the love of God in Christ as reaching out to the whole world. Our universal connectedness allows love to spread from one being and one part of creation to another, until eventually love gathers us up into ultimate fulfilment in God. In this passage, Teilhard imagines God speaking to Elijah in the desert:

'The supreme key to the enigma, the dazzling utterance which is inscribed on my brow and which henceforth will burn into your eyes even though you close them, is this: *Nothing is precious save what is yourself in others and others in yourself.* In heaven, all things are but one. In heaven all is one.'[5]

The more we understand that we are one body, the less we think in individualistic terms, of our own needs and desires, and the more we think of the needs and desires of all human beings, and ultimately of the whole of creation.

So, finally, in the Pentecost discussion group we reached an answer to our first question, What is love? Love, we felt, is first of all the recognition that we are one – one kin, one body – as human beings, and as part of God's creation. We belong together. We are part of one another, because no one develops as a human being apart from other human beings.

As human beings, we want and hope for many of the same things – enough to eat and drink; freedom from conflict; love, happiness and fulfilment. Love understands that if we hope for these things for ourselves, we must help to create them for others. No one can thrive unless everyone thrives. Love acts on that understanding, doing what makes ourselves and others thrive as human beings, and avoiding what hurts and damages us.

Love looks at the world it belongs to, and is glad to be part of it. It doesn't want to cut itself off from the rest of creation, but is committed to living fully within it, sharing its life, and helping to give life more abundantly.

Love recognizes that the world is damaged by the hurt we have done to one another in the past. It chooses not to pass on that damage but, guided by the teaching of Jesus Christ, to try to create a better environment, more harmonious communities and more loving relationships in the future.

Love and the threefold God

The group reached this conclusion by thinking about family love and neighbourliness, but we could have approached it equally well from a different starting point.

Christian teaching speaks of God as both One and Three: as a plurality in perfect harmony with itself. God as Creator, God in Jesus Christ and the Spirit of God may relate to us in different ways, but in themselves they are indivisible: one God. And as each of us is said to be made in the image of God, so our human plurality is also, ultimately, a unity, and ideally exists in harmony.

In practice, though, we often strain and damage our relationships, our harmony with each other and with God, by hurting one another, or by ignoring or not attending to one another.

The experience of the followers of Jesus Christ was that a loving God had reached out, through Christ, to heal us and our relationships, and reconcile us with one another and with Godself. 'In Christ,' as Paul says (2 Cor. 5.19), 'God was reconciling the world to himself.' That experience of divine love, coupled with our own experience and our trust in God, is the basis for our conviction that the work of love is to restore unity and harmony to the world, among human beings and between human beings and God.

The central part love plays in our understanding of God's relationship with us is vividly expressed in the many great Christian hymns about love. In this one, Charles Wesley describes how love flows from God to us, making us more loveable, enabling us to love one another, and ultimately uniting us all with God:

> Love divine, all loves excelling,
> joy of heaven, to earth come down,
> fix in us thy humble dwelling,
> all thy faithful mercies crown.
>
> Jesu, thou art all compassion,
> pure unbounded love thou art:
> visit us with they salvation,
> enter ev'ry trembling heart.
>
> Breathe, O breathe thy loving Sprit
> into ev'ry troubled breast;
> let us all in thee inherit,
> let us find thy promised rest.
>
> Take away the love of sinning,
> Alpha and Omega be;
> end of faith, as its beginning,
> set our hearts at liberty . . .

Finish then thy new creation,
pure and spotless let us be;
let us see thy great salvation
perfectly restored in thee.

Changed from glory into glory,
till in heav'n we take our place,
till we cast our crowns before thee,
lost in wonder, love, and praise.

The New Testament describes how God loves creation with the love of a parent for the family he has created. Jesus Christ loves his fellow human beings with the love of a man who knows that he is God's son, and brother to God's children. When we recognize that we are one body, we are following the example of Jesus (an idea we shall return to in Chapter 5), and loving one another in the way that God loves us.

Love as self-sacrifice

At this point, one member of the discussion group pointed out that we had not yet mentioned self-sacrifice, which many people see as central to Christian love. So we spent some time reflecting on self-sacrifice or self-giving.

The Gospels suggest that Jesus saw his own death as a voluntary sacrifice, in which his death would act as a ransom, freeing human souls from some kind of bondage (e.g. Mark 10.45), or (through the shedding of his blood, like that of a sacrificial animal) as the symbolic seal of a new covenant between God and humanity (e.g. Matt. 26.28).[6] The idea that Jesus' self-sacrifice 'saved' humanity was central to the faith of the first Christians, and it appears in most of the books of the New Testament, though they don't explore in detail how we are saved.[7] The writers of the New Testament also affirm that the sacrifice of Christ reconciled humanity to God, restoring us to a loving relationship from which we had turned away (e.g. 2 Cor. 5.18–19), though again, they do not explain exactly how.

Jesus several times invites us to follow his example: 'If any want to become my followers, let them deny themselves and take up their cross and follow me. For those who want to save their life will lose it, and those who lose their life for my sake, and for the sake of the gospel, will save it' (Mark 8.34–35). Many Christians have seen self-sacrifice as an important part of their self-dedication to Christ: as a privilege and a joy, even when it has led to suffering and death.

Self-sacrifice can also, though, be badly misunderstood. It can be invoked in a spirit of joyless and destructive self-pity: 'Oh, don't mind me, trample all over me, *I* don't matter . . .' It can be used to justify one person's being made miserable so that another can be happy. At the extreme, it has been used to tell slaves that they should be grateful to be able to serve their masters, women that they should feel privileged to serve men, and members of one culture that they must serve another.

The group agreed that any understanding of self-sacrifice which involves telling other people that they should sacrifice themselves for us, must be wrong. It may be a loving action to lay down one's life for a friend; it is not loving to try to get a friend to lay down their life for oneself. Hurting or destroying another person for our own benefit makes a mockery of divine love, which loves and values all beings equally.

There are many ways of trying to understand the nature and effect of Jesus' self-sacrifice for us, but they are all based on two things: Jesus' self-sacrifice was voluntary, and it was undertaken in the conviction that only good would come of it. Even Jesus himself is not ultimately destroyed by his sacrifice. By speaking of his divinity, his resurrection and his ascension into heaven, the New Testament, and later reflections on it, affirm that Christ's self-sacrifice, though it led to his death, was not a form of self-destruction.

Using the language of love, we might tentatively expand that affirmation as follows. One of the extraordinary qualities of Jesus Christ was his understanding of the unity of all beings with one another. He perceived that he himself, in life and even in death, was indivisibly part of the oneness of creation. Love was his gift to the world, and by choosing to love even those who put him to death, he planted his love in their hearts like a seed in fertile ground. Only his body was destroyed by death; his love continued to live in the lives of those who had encountered him and were transformed by his love, and in God, from whom he knew that neither life nor death can part us.

If we say this much, then we are beginning to think about the nature of atonement: *how*, as Christians proclaim, Jesus Christ saves us. This is a complex and difficult question, to which many answers have been offered, and none universally accepted. But following the lines of thought which have brought us this far, we may try to outline the saving quality of Christ a little further.

As a human being, Jesus was shaped, like all of us, by his family, friends and environment. But he had the divine quality of not being damaged by our damaged world. He knew and experienced the prejudices of his society, the hurtful passions and shortcomings of the people around him, but he did not respond by allowing himself to be damaged or turning to hurt other people. He had the divine gift of understanding, the ability to look deeply into other people and see not only how they were damaged, but also their good qualities – the seeds of love, trust and hope inside them.

Reaching out to the people he encountered, Jesus met their hurt with love, and fostered their strengths and goodness, helping them to heal. He comprehended the harm they were capable of doing, and gave them a safe and loving space in which to change. This gift is what we call forgiveness. By his death, and appearances to his followers after his death, he showed that even death does not destroy such deep love and understanding, such forgiveness and healing, once it has been in the world.

Jesus made his followers understand that having been touched and changed by him, they carried him in their hearts and minds, bodies and souls, and could continue his work of love and pass it on to others. Once we have been touched by a love which understands our hurt but is not damaged by it, which gives us a space to be forgiven and heal, we cannot help being changed. Even though Jesus the man is not alive on earth now, the effects of his life and his spirit are unquenchable.

There are many ways to express our love for others by giving our lives for them. We may look after them, work on their behalf, speak out for them, teach them, pray for them, even die for them. If we give our lives in the conviction that we are one body, and that what we do for someone else benefits the whole world, then we are following Christ. If our own or anyone else's suffering benefits some people at the expense of others, then it is not the transformative suffering of Christ, but only the outworking of somebody's selfishness. The sacrifice of anyone is only justifiable if it is real self-sacrifice, an act of love, undertaken to bring healing to the world.

Judging whether an act of self-sacrifice is justifiable or not takes care and practice. The same act may be appropriate in some circumstances and not in others. If I choose to devote my life to looking after my sister because she is researching a cure for cancer, that may be absolutely right. If I choose to do the same because she wants me to and has always told me what to do, it may not be right.

This is perhaps why early Christian codes of conduct often don't say much about specific actions. It's always right to help the weak and vulnerable, and not to lie, steal, murder, worship idols or commit adultery, but beyond that, we tend to be told not specifically what to do, but how to do it. So, for instance, in Galatians, Paul tells his community to bear the fruits of the Spirit: love, joy, peace, patience, kindness, generosity, faithfulness, gentleness and self-control (5.22–23). The specific actions we perform are less important than the kind of good, harmonious, hopeful community they produce.

Who should we love?

The second question which the Pentecost group wanted to discuss was, Who should we love? We were surprised to find how many different answers Christians have given to it.

At one extreme are Jesus' words in the Sermon on the Mount (Matt. 5.43–47):

> 'You have heard that it was said, "You shall love your neighbour and hate your enemy." But I say to you, Love your enemies and pray for those who persecute you, so that you may be children of your Father in heaven; for he makes his sun rise on the evil and on the good, and sends rain on the righteous and on the unrighteous.'

This saying is part of a passage in which Jesus is urging his followers to do more than keep the letter of religious law. The law, for example, tells us not to commit murder, but we should not even be angry with others.

This saying on love is not cited very often in writers of the first few centuries of the Church.[8] It seems that most early Christians found the idea of loving everyone too much of a challenge. It has, though, become very popular in the last century or so.

Many people nowadays would cite the parable of the Good Samaritan (Luke 10.29–37) as their guide to who to love. The Samaritan acted as a neighbour to the man who needed him, despite the fact that they belonged to rather different communities, and ones which did not get on well. We can take this parable in the same spirit as Matthew 5.43–47, as meaning that we should love everyone. Alternatively, we could take it as meaning that we can act as neighbours towards *anyone*, but we do not necessarily have to be neighbourly towards *everyone*. It could even mean that we only need be neighbourly when people are in need, and not the rest of the time.

In the early Church, perhaps the most popular understanding of love was that Christians only needed to love other Christians. St John's Gospel seems to tend in this direction. Although John says that God so loved the world that he sent Christ into it, he never seems to expect the whole world to respond. Instead, he describes Christians as a small group who show their love for Christ by loving one another, and brace themselves to withstand the hatred of the rest of the world:

'If the world hates you, be aware that it hated me before it hated you. If you belonged to the world, the world would love you as its own. Because you do not belong to the world, but I have chosen you out of the world – therefore the world hates you.'   (John. 15.18–19)

In parts, the book of Revelation seems to be even more exclusive. According to one of the author's visions, the number of those who will go to heaven is symbolically fixed from the foundation of the world. There are 144,000 of them, and the seal of God is on their foreheads (7.3–4). If one is not one of the chosen, presumably one need not even hope to be loved by those who are.

The Acts of the Apostles takes a different view again. Some of the most moving passages of Acts (4.32–37; 6.1–6) are about how the first Christians take care of one another, especially of those, like widows and orphans, who are the most vulnerable in society. But the first Christians are also interested in anyone who might want to join the community, and the apostles welcome all those who come to them to be healed or taught. Many people since have felt that this was a helpful interpretation of Christian love: that we should love those who are already Christians, and those who might be about to become Christians.

From the beginning of the tradition, therefore, there has been no one answer to the question of who we should love. There is a case, though, for seeing an implicit, if not an explicit answer running through most of the New Testament, and it is the answer of the Sermon on the Mount. If we do not love other people, then our relationship with them is at best one of indifference, and at worst one of envy, contempt, dislike or even hatred, all of which damage ourselves and others and lead to conflict, unhappiness and further damage. The New Testament tells us repeatedly that all those behaviours are a failure of love, and always wrong.

The discussion concluded that the only course which the New Testament really commends, is that we love everyone.

How should we love?

Last but not least, our group reflected on how we could put love into practice every day in the places where we lived and worked. The good news about *agape*, we felt, is that everyday life is full of opportunities to express it.

Several members of the group were spending a lot of time looking after their grandchildren, while their children were at work – a pattern which has become increasingly common in recent years. Grandparents always say how much they enjoy it, but it is also an act of great love, especially when the grandparents themselves may recently have retired from work, and may be looking forward to having a bit more time to relax and look after themselves and each other.

I am often impressed by the *agape* of my students, who spend a substantial portion of their free time doing voluntary work. Some of them act as peer supporters and welfare officers for their fellow students. Others help with reading practice in a local primary school; others again help to run holiday camps or summer schools for less privileged children.

Several of us agreed that we express love towards our colleagues at work by being efficient administrators. Answering emails as soon as possible shows that one respects the sender and does not want to make their life difficult or frustrating. Chairing a meeting efficiently means that everyone gets to go home sooner. Doing the jobs one is asked to do, promptly and carefully, enables other people to do their jobs more easily. In the large, complex organizations in which so many of us work, a good administrator is a good shepherd to their colleagues – creating an environment in which everyone can thrive and do their job well.

Many workplaces demand a lot of their employees nowadays, and are not always very sympathetic if people are ill, or distracted by personal problems, or just not as quick or efficient as their fellow-workers. Here again is an opportunity for *agape*. We need, of course, to be aware of both sides of any problem. Employers have targets and deadlines to meet and financial strictures and obligations. Employees are human beings and not just parts of a machine. But within those constraints, there can be space for negotiation and kindness. If we are working with someone who is struggling, perhaps we can help in some practical way. If our own performance is below par, we might consider whether we are being fair to our employer. If we are the employer, we might find out what the problem is and whether we can help solve it.

In all kinds of situations, we express love for the people around us by remembering that nobody's life is simple, and that even people we know well may be suffering stresses and strains we don't know about. When people are difficult or irritable or let us down, it is always worth cutting them a bit of slack – giving them the benefit of the doubt – asking how they are rather than grumbling behind their back.

Even getting from one place to another gives us an opportunity to practise *agape*. Few things, the group agreed, damage the quality of everyday life more than the frustration and anger which road – and even pavement – users so often offload on one another. Everyone sees themselves as a victim and everyone else as an abuser. But very few people really mean to be inconsiderate or put others in danger. People get tired and stressed; they're frequently in a hurry; they make mistakes. We are all victims to some extent of a society to which we all also contribute, which encourages us to dash everywhere and resent anything or anyone that gets in our way.

Rather than getting angry, we might practise loving our fellow road users. Keeping calm helps other people to keep calm. Giving people the space and time they need to get where they are going keeps everyone safe. Affirming by the way we drive or walk that other people have the same right to be there as we do ourselves, helps them feel less like victims, and makes it easier for them to be calm and generous in turn.

Whenever we testify by our actions that we are one creation, all interconnected, then we are practising *agape*. Whenever we help ourselves to thrive, to be happy and fulfilled, by helping others to thrive and be happy and fulfilled, then we are practising love.

Whenever we try not to add to the hurt and damage in the world, then we are practising *agape.*

Our Pentecost group came to see all the activities which we discussed in the rest of our meetings as aspects of love: listening to people, speaking or acting for those who need our help, working to bring about reconciliation and forgiveness, talking to fellow explorers in faith or defusing those unhelpful qualities in us which hinder our ministry to others. Whenever we minister to anyone in any form, we concluded, we are practising *agape.*

Questions for discussion

- Who do you love?
- Who do you think you should love?
- Who would you like to be able to love?
- How do you love?

2

Attentiveness: the ministry of listening

———•◆•———

Having explored the meaning of Christian love, the Pentecost group turned next to one of the simplest and most powerful ways in which we can offer love to individual people: by listening to them.

After food, shelter and safety, the most basic necessities of life, nothing matters more to human beings than attention. To be seen and heard – to have our presence in the world marked – is a universal and fundamental need. When we are babies and small children, the response of people around us teaches us that we belong to the same species and group. Gradually, we discover that the noises we make, the words we speak, the way we act, all have different and specific effects on others. We are part of a community. Being part of a community gives us a sense of substance and significance. We affect the world around us and are affected by it: we matter.

The older we grow, the more we find that words and actions have different effects in different situations. Human community is complex and densely woven, and our place in it varies according to what we are doing and with whom. As long as we know we matter, we can take on all sorts of roles and make many different kinds of relationships. If we lack that basic sense, we will probably find it much harder to play a full part in our community and make good relationships.

When people don't pay enough attention to babies and children, some grow up feeling that they don't quite exist – that they are not quite as solid, as visible or audible as other people, and can't make as much impact on the world around them. Others start to seek attention by making too much or the wrong kind of impact. Others again develop too little respect for community members: their property, needs, values, friendship or love.

Even when people have been given plenty of attention as they were growing up, and have a healthy sense that they are a significant part of a community, that sense can be damaged later in life. When we are elderly or ill, for example, if we need to be looked after in an institution, it's often hard to feel that we're still part of a community. If we spend a lot of time looking after other people, we may get so used to giving care and attention that we lose the sense that we are receiving it, or enough of it. When that happens, our sense of self is diminished, along with our sense of community, and we are in danger of passing our loss of connectedness on to others.

We don't have to be ill, elderly or frail to feel the pressures of life fraying our sense of self and community. Even those who are young, healthy and have lots of friends can develop a feeling that they are not being heard, or not making an impact. The modern world tells us to search relentlessly for self-fulfilment; to work, play, shop, travel, party, blog and tweet – all with a view to our own self-realization and satisfaction. Other people's fulfilment is regarded as their problem, not ours. As a result, while most people love to think and talk about themselves, few have much sense of the effects of their talk on others, or spend as much time listening as talking.

To form part of a good community, the group agreed, we need to experience both our impact upon other people, and theirs on us. If we don't, then no matter how busy we are or how loudly we talk, in the end we will lose our sense of connectedness. And then we'll begin to feel lost, in a world without the structure and support of relationships.

Good relationships, good communities, a good environment – all exist in balance: giving and taking, talking and listening, acting and letting ourselves be acted on. We all need to sound off occasionally about what frustrates or upsets us; to celebrate what we love; to mull over our experiences, at a profound or just an everyday level. Equally, we need to recognize that other people need to do the same. It's important to take time to help each other register our significance in the world: to attend. With that thought in mind, the Pentecost group began to think about attentiveness, beginning with some passages from the Bible.

Attentiveness in the New Testament

The call to attentiveness is everywhere in the New Testament, though it is not always explicit. We see it in the way Jesus is always prepared to be waylaid, and to listen to the needs of people who came to him. Again and again in the Gospels, Jesus is teaching, or on his way somewhere, when someone interrupts him, asking for help for him- or herself or a friend or relative. Jesus' attention is immediately, wholly on that person: he sees and hears him or her and perceives what needs to be done. Even when he does not see someone approach him, he is so sensitive to the people around him that he knows when he has been touched.

When the woman with the haemorrhage touches Jesus' cloak from behind in the crowd (Mark 5.25–34), he feels power go out of him and turns to ask, 'Who has touched my clothes?' The disciples say, look at the crowd! Any number of people could have touched you! But Jesus persists, looking for the particular person who touched him in a particular way. When she eventually approaches him, trembling with fear, he recognizes her distress and says gently, 'Daughter, your faith has made you well; go in peace, and be healed of your disease.'

Jesus' attentiveness to people, as the Gospel-writers describe it, means that he often sees something in them which no one else notices. How does Jesus know that the hated tax collector sitting at his customs post will make a good disciple (Mark 2.13–14)? How does he know that Peter, despite his limited understanding of Jesus in his lifetime, will become a rock on which the future Christian community can stand firm (Matt. 16.17–19)? He looks deeply into them and sees more than others see.

In the Epistles, the earliest Christians are constantly encouraged to be attentive towards one another. It is part of loving one another and forging a community of faith. We are one body, Paul tells the Romans and the Corinthians, with different gifts and different roles to play. To work well together we need to discern what gifts people have and let them use them.[1] Paul urges the Romans to be aware of both the nature and the situation of those around them: 'Rejoice with those who rejoice, weep with those who weep . . .' (Rom. 12.15).

'Bear one another's burdens', says Paul to the Galatians (6.2), while he advises the Thessalonians (1 Thess. 5.14), 'Admonish the idlers, encourage the faint-hearted, help the weak, be patient with all of them.' The Letter of James warns Christians not to judge people by appearances, but honour them for who they really are: '[I]f a person with gold rings and in fine clothes comes into your assembly, and if a poor person in dirty clothes also comes in, and if you take notice of the one wearing the fine clothes and say, "Have a seat here, please", while to the one who is poor you say, "Stand there", or, "Sit at my feet", have you not made distinctions among yourselves, and become judges with evil thoughts?' (James 2.2–4). The First Letter of Peter (1 Pet. 3.8) urges that we exercise sympathy for one another, 'All of you, have unity of spirit, sympathy, love for one another, a tender heart, and a humble mind.'

The practice of listening

Being attentive towards other people, aware of their situation and their needs, and of our effect on one another, is something we can all practise every day. The group thought that the easiest way to begin was simply by being prepared to listen. Listening is pure attentiveness, and is one of the most loving and most helpful things we can do for each other.

It takes practice, of course. Listening is time-consuming, and we can't always predict when someone will need to talk. If we are serious about it, we have to build a certain amount of flexibility into our everyday lives. It's no use wanting to be there for people, if in practice we're always busy when they need us.

People in need tend to have sound instincts about who will be a good listener and who won't. Being available in principle, and even having a certain amount of free time, is a good start, but we also need to be approachable. People have to feel that they can trust us. It helps to present an open and gentle face to the world. People who listen need to be discreet and not to rush into judgement. People who are obviously busy or impatient, who enjoy gossip, who have a reputation for liking to tell people what to do, or who are felt to be narrow-minded or judgemental, are all likely to be avoided by people in need. Above all, we need to be aware of others as we go about our daily business, in order that when they need us, we are attending and can respond appropriately.

In the years since I was ordained, I have been caught out many times by not being attentive enough at the moment when someone needed to speak. On one occasion, the chaplain of my college was rushed to hospital, seriously ill, right at the start of the university term. I offered to take the chapel services while he was away. I had not bargained for the possibility that once the students saw me acting as chaplain, some of them would also want to talk.

They would turn up at my office at all hours of the day, walk in uninvited and sit down, and start to tell me about whatever was troubling them, while I stared at them in consternation. I was still doing my regular job: I had students to teach, papers to write, meetings to go to . . . I just didn't have time – or rather, I had not built any flexibility into my schedule – to fit in people who needed to be listened to. In the six weeks I acted as chaplain, I never did make enough time. I ended up working half the night to keep up with my job, and I can't think that the quality of my listening (accompanied as it was by the deafening tick of an imaginary clock in my head) helped anyone much. It was a painful and salutary experience.

Many people are naturally good listeners, and most people can listen in some situations. When we start to practise listening regularly, we all have some experience to draw on. The people we find it easiest to listen to are probably the people to whom we naturally listen most attentively. We'll probably find that our posture, as we listen to them, is very open. We don't turn away from them, or hide our faces with a hand or strand of hair. We probably don't fold our arms – a classic sign that one is not feeling very accessible.

When we're listening well, we often nod from time to time and make quiet, half-articulate sounds of encouragement (mmm . . . yes . . .). Good listeners often instinctively 'reflect' what people say back to them, by quietly repeating their words or paraphrasing them. This shows that one is attending, and tells the other person that one can see their point of view. (Professional counsellors do this too.) Reflecting can also help the speaker to focus and clarify their thinking, because when we hear our own words repeated in someone else's voice, we become more aware of what we are saying.

Above all, the discussion group agreed, when we are listening to people, we need to *listen*, and *not* to talk. Listening is about the other person, not about ourselves. When someone needs to talk, let them talk!

While I was training for ordination, I spent several months visiting one afternoon a week at a local hospital. I was given a floor and told to visit each ward, to say hello to people and see who wanted to talk. I was very nervous about walking into a room full of strangers, but I soon found that most people were glad of any company.

At first, as they talked about their experiences, I would sometimes try to show that I understood by telling some similar story from my own life. I quickly discovered that this only annoyed people and put them off. I wasn't there to talk, but to listen. If I'd had similar experiences, they didn't need to know about them. What they needed was for me to hear their story. Often I didn't understand it – I didn't yet know what it was like to be very elderly, or seriously ill, or to lose a parent or a child. As it turned out, that didn't matter very much. What mattered was that I listened to what people said.

I came to see the listener's role as twofold. Simply being there allows people to articulate their experience, which may help them to get to grips with it, make sense of it, think through it, or begin to come to terms with it. But the listener also represents the rest of the world.

If we visit a hospital, for instance, we help to give the patients, marooned as they are on the desert island of their ward, a sense that they are still connected. The world out there knows they are here. It cares. It has sent someone to keep in touch. When we leave, we will take what we have heard with us, and the world will know what is happening to those inside. It doesn't even matter if we don't know people's families, neighbours or friends, if we only meet them once, or if we're not charged with telling their story to anyone in particular. Our being there and listening is a connection, and that's important in itself.

The group discussed a passage from Neil Belton's biography of Helen Bamber, the founder of the Medical Foundation for the Care of the Victims of Torture. Bamber was a passionate and influential campaigner against regimes which practise torture, and few people have more vividly understood the importance of listening as part of a process by which human beings mutilated by suffering can begin the long journey towards healing. Listening was, and is, central to the work of the Foundation.

Through being listened to, people who have been brutally damaged may begin to face their experience and come to grips with it. They are given a chance to take some control over their memories. They may even come to feel that they can move on from their experience or in some way make use of it. Ultimately, listening may become a means by which trust in other people and hope for the future are restored to people from whom they have been violently stolen.

Bamber's life's work of listening to people who had undergone unimaginable suffering began in 1945, when, at the age of 20, she joined the Jewish Relief Unit in London and travelled to the newly liberated Belsen concentration camp. She quickly discovered that one of the things survivors of the camp most needed was to speak about what had happened to them, and that she had a rare capacity to listen.

> Above all else, there was the need to tell you *everything*, over and over and over again. And this was the most significant thing for me, realizing that you had to take it all. They would need to hold onto you, and many of them still had very thin arms . . . hands almost like claws, and they would hold you, and it was important that you held them, and often you had to rock, there was a rocking, bowing movement, as you sat on the floor – there was very little to sit on – and you would hold onto them and they would tell you their story. Sometimes it was in Yiddish, and although I had learned some, it was as though you didn't really need a language. It took me a long time to realize that you couldn't really do anything but that you just had to hang onto them and that you had to listen and to *receive* this, as if it belonged partly to you, and in that act of taking and showing that you were available you were playing some useful role.[2]

The need to speak and be heard, which Bamber discovered in the concentration camp, is part of human nature and all human communities. We meet it constantly, in much more humdrum forms, in everyday life.

Pitfalls, scapegoats and boundaries

The group all agreed that – however difficult it is – when we listen to people, it is important to resist the urge to offer advice. Unless we're asked for it explicitly (and sometimes even then), advice can sound dangerously like judgement to someone who is feeling vulnerable. Listening involves putting ourselves in the speaker's place, and trying to see their situation from their perspective. If it isn't helpful to offer advice, though, it may be helpful to note our own reactions to what we hear. They tell us a lot about ourselves – our weaknesses, our vulnerabilities, our assumptions, the areas where we find it easy to sympathize and the ones where we don't. This teaches us about the parts our own lives which need attention, if we are to grow in sympathy and compassion for others.

In the book of Job, Job's friends are notorious examples of pastoral blunderers, who make all the mistakes of the poor listener. To be fair, they seem to mean well, and they start quite well too. All three – Eliphaz, Bildad and Zophar – journey long distances to be with Job when they hear that he has lost his wealth, family and health. When they see him sitting in the ashes, they weep aloud and join him on the ground, and for seven days and nights, they accompany him in his suffering without saying a word. When finally Job speaks, they hear him out.

So far, so good. Then (Ch. 4) Eliphaz asks Job, sympathetically, whether it is all right to speak. He affirms Job's history as a strong and wise man. But then he starts criticizing. Shouldn't Job's wisdom, his piety, his integrity of life, be a resource? Should Job not trust that God will not allow an innocent man to die? Eliphaz tells Job that a word has come to Eliphaz himself in the night, as a result of which he is in a position to advise Job. The word said (4.17), 'Can mortals be righteous before God? Can human beings be pure before their Maker?' No! God can find fault with anyone, and when he does he may destroy them utterly.

This passage, in which Eliphaz boasts of his revelation, gives unwanted advice, and seems to tell Job that his suffering must be his own fault, is about as unhelpful as it is possible to be. Even the fact that what Eliphaz tells Job – no one is righteous before God – is close to what Job eventually comes to believe himself, doesn't improve things. It almost never helps to tell someone something which they're not yet ready to hear. Job's comforters are a cautionary tale for would-be listeners – not because they are bad people, because they're not – not even because they get everything wrong, because they don't – but because they show how easy it is, even when one has many of the right instincts and begins well, to sabotage a caring relationship with one or two ill-judged remarks.

People who are good listeners do more than their share of it, and it's an occupational hazard of being a good listener that sometimes people abuse one's goodwill. Some people like to talk about themselves, whether or not they have any particular problems. Others just want to gossip or grumble about a mutual acquaintance. If we're committed to listening, we have to accept that sometimes it won't be very productive. But it's better to be there sometimes for people who don't really need us, than to risk not being there for the person who really does.

Occasionally, after talking about something painful or personal, the speaker will push the listener away. The reason may simply be embarrassment, but often it is something more profound. When we listen, we take on something of the other person's problems and burdens. Their instinct is then sometimes to drive us away, and their problems with us. We may remember the way ancient Israelites, once a year, chose a goat, the 'scapegoat', loaded it symbolically with their sins, and drove it out into the desert. Sometimes we become, in that ancient sense, another person's scapegoat. When that happens, there is nothing to do but accept it. Sometimes, after a while, the person will receive us back into friendship. Sometimes they never will.

Occasionally, someone who wants to talk is in very serious emotional or psychological distress, and then we have to decide whether to suggest that he or she seeks help elsewhere. One doesn't have to be a trained counsellor or psychiatrist to be a good listener, but one does have to develop a sense of what is beyond one's capacity to handle. Intimately interrelated and involved as all living beings are, everyone to whom we listen has an impact on us, just as we hope to have (or mediate) an effect on them. Sometimes their distress may be too much for us to hold.

When we feel overwhelmed by something we hear, we remember that it isn't we ourselves who hope to heal our neighbours, but Christ in us, whose healing power is infinitely greater than ours, and who can't be damaged by their damage. We also remind ourselves that although we are called to love our neighbours, we're not called to love their failings, and it's right and natural to be upset by deep unhappiness, put off by destructive behaviour, and horrified by evil. It's also important to recognize where our individual limitations are. If someone who comes to talk to us is so distressed, so damaged or so damaging that we think we can't help, and he or she is likely to do harm to us, then we may have to suggest that he or she talks to someone else.

When we believe that we can help someone, we still have to learn, by trial and error, how much time it's appropriate to give to any one person. People take very different approaches to managing their time, which to some extent are a matter of temperament. Discussing pastoral ministry with a clerical colleague, I once observed that I was willing to spend as much time listening as my other commitments (which, unfortunately, are often too many) would allow. He took the opposite view. 'You've got to have boundaries', he said firmly. 'Anyone who comes to see me gets an hour. No more.' There was a respectful pause while we contemplated his self-discipline. 'Of course,' he said thoughtfully, 'an hour doesn't necessarily mean an *hour*. Sometimes it means two or three.'

Distinctively Christian listening

Professional counsellors and therapists typically spend about an hour at a time with their patients, and may meet them regularly over long periods. The structure of religious listening tends to be more varied and informal. As we practise listening as Christians, it is worth reflecting on the differences between what counsellors and therapists do and what we are trying to do.

Anne Long is an Anglican priest and a consultant with the Acorn Christian Healing Trust, who has written books on pastoral care and spiritual direction. In her book *Listening*, she explores what is distinctive about the Christian ministry of listening. She suggests that what makes Christian listeners distinctive is their experience, which other people instinctively respond to, that Christ is at the centre of their own lives and their listening to others. Christian listeners point beyond themselves to the grace of God, which has the capacity to transform all lives. They develop this quality of pointing towards God, and acting as a sign of God's presence, through their own prayer lives. 'Above all,' says Long, 'the Christian listener is to be a "living reminder" of God and one whose whole life incarnates the gifts and graces of Christ.'[3]

The quality of pointing beyond oneself to God and to Christ is central to what it means to live a Christian life. It expresses our sense that whatever we are able to do for others is not solely the fruit of our own human nature and experience, nor even the experience of our culture or humanity as a whole. Remarkable as human nature is, and varied as human experience is, humanity is too small and shallow a spiritual pool to heal its own self-inflicted wounds and those of the world.

What human beings mediate in our moments of grace are the qualities of the far deeper and more powerful nature of God. The nature of God can't be damaged by rejection. It forgives, and its forgiveness isn't worn out by indifference. It hopes, and its hope is never soured by disappointment. Christians know that the love and hopefulness and grace of God are always and unchangeably there for us, ready to embrace and transform us, whenever we allow ourselves to turn to God.

Step by step, as our faith develops, we allow ourselves to accept that embrace, and are more and more transformed by it. This gives us a security, an unshakable sense of being known and loved, valued and inspired, which helps us to be more loving, more giving, more forgiving, more hopeful on behalf of others than our limited hearts and minds could ever be by themselves. At their best, therefore, Christian listeners help to channel divine healing into the world, with its infinite possibilities for transformation and regeneration through hope and love.

Most Christian listeners do not have professional qualifications. But that too has advantages: above all, that our listening is that of friends and neighbours. We are not called to perform a service for people which ends when the hour or the course of treatment ends. We are called to love people as people, as fellow children of God, and wherever possible to make our listening to them part of an authentic relationship. And because we're in a relationship, it's also important to remember that we're not only giving something to the other person, we're also receiving something – trust, affection or affirmation – which is a gift in its own right.

To be a good listener, it certainly helps to like people, and to find people interesting. At the same time, not everyone we listen to will be a natural friend or companion. Accepting those we don't instinctively warm to as part of our lives is also part of what it means to be a good neighbour. When we're listening to someone who isn't a natural soulmate, it's important to remember that we're always receiving as well as giving something as we listen, and to reflect on what that is.

Bill Kirkpatrick is an Anglican priest who has developed a ministry of listening over many years, and has written extensively about different aspects of pastoral ministry. In *The Creativity of Listening*, he explores further the idea that we both give and receive something when we listen:

> I suspect that, like myself, many involved in the ministry of care are doing so because of their own healing needs. Provided that these needs are not greater than those of the person we are caring for (or with), then the channel of the healing grace of God is released in a way which is beneficial for all involved. We learn to care through having been cared for, and it is through caring that we learn how to be co-caring of each other . . .
>
> There is no doubt that both listener and speaker are offering as well as receiving. When this is recognized, we are able to release together the healing energies latent within ourselves. As listener and speaker we both offer and receive care. I try to offer all of myself, through my presence and the attentiveness of my hearing through listening, to the all-ness of the speaker. A similar activity flows from the speaker to myself.[4]

If we recognize that we are one body, inextricably linked in one creation, and that we can't flourish alone, but only together, then it becomes obvious why it is important to listen, with love, to anyone and everyone who needs us, and to accept that in giving our time and attention we are also receiving something from the other person. We fulfil our potential as God's creation not alone, but in partnership with all created beings.

At the end of our discussion of listening, some of the members of the Pentecost group pointed out that however much we want to attend to people and to act as 'living reminders' of God and Christ, we often get in our own way. Most of us are at best extremely imperfect channels for the Holy Spirit: leaky pipes, obstructed by the twists and turns of our own personalities, and clogged with residual insecurities, fears, angers and desires. As we try to share the grace of God with others, we know we are very much in need of grace ourselves. Alongside our listening, therefore, we need to try to defuse those things in ourselves which obstruct the action of the Spirit in us. How we do that is the subject of Chapter 5. At the same time, we agreed that listening to people is also good practice for listening to God, which is the theme of Chapter 6.

Questions for discussion

- Do you find listening easy? Difficult? Rewarding? Frustrating?
- Does your listening change as you do more of it?
- What are the dangers for the listener? What are the rewards?

3

The call to prophecy

The Pentecost discussion group spent three meetings reflecting on how important it is to love one another and to be attentive to one another. We are one body, and no part of the body of a community, a society or creation as a whole, flourishes to the full unless every part is flourishing. We found it relatively easy to agree on that, but our next session took us to a topic which proved more difficult and more controversial: prophecy. I hoped to persuade the group that prophets too practise love and attentiveness. They tend to do it, though, towards communities as a whole, and with a particular purpose: to identify how a community is failing in love, and suggest ways for it to change.

When biblical prophets hear and answer the call of God, they begin a journey which takes them beyond the boundaries of their community, and helps them to see it from God's perspective. Some, like Elijah, spend time physically away from society, in the desert; others, like Ezekiel and Jonah, abandon their job, home and social status. In the process, they step out of their inherited assumptions and conventional patterns of thought. They see the world afresh. Often what they see makes them deeply critical. Sometimes it discourages them profoundly. Sometimes it enables them to see wonders invisible to others. The prophet Anna, for instance, in Luke's Gospel, is one of the few people who recognize the baby Jesus as the Messiah.

The call to prophecy is a call to stand with one foot outside our ordinary lives, our everyday activities and assumptions, and see them as God and Christ might see them. Are we behaving as if we love one another? Are the structures we build around ourselves – political, social, economic, cultural – founded on love? Are the places where we live and work fit for God's children? Are they treated with justice and respect? If not, why not?

The challenge of prophecy

> Now the word of the LORD came to Jonah son of Amittai, saying, 'Go at once to Nineveh, that great city, and cry out against it; for their wickedness has come up before me.' But Jonah set out to flee to Tarshish from the presence of the LORD . . .' (Jonah 1.1–3)

The group agreed that there is a certain glamour about the great prophets of the Bible – an aura of holiness and power. But the idea that we might be called to prophecy ourselves was a very different matter, and to many of us not at all welcome. Prophets have to push themselves forward. They have to speak out, which nearly always causes trouble. They attract attention, which is all too often hostile. Their mission is likely to disrupt their life, if it doesn't completely take it over. They sometimes end up being persecuted, even killed. None of us had any ambition to cause that much trouble or attract that kind of attention. We sympathized with Jonah who, when the word of the Lord came to him telling him to prophesy against Ninevah, ran away.

One member of the group observed that people who speak out are likely to be rather different in character from those who are good listeners – and being a good listener, we had agreed, was very important. Another pointed out that most of us weren't in a good position to tackle the big problems of our society: we lacked the experience or the qualifications.

Prophetic ministry is a challenge – any ministry is a challenge. It may well take us out of our comfort zone – intellectually, socially and spiritually. But I suspect that we are often more nervous of it than we need be. The group looked at the careers of one biblical and several modern prophets, which show that prophecy is a much more varied ministry than we might think. It isn't always negative and confrontational, but often involves a lot of listening and dialogue. It doesn't usually wrench people out of their current way of life; more often it emerges out of everyday experience, and develops hand in hand with it. And the rewards of prophetic ministry are very great. It deepens our understanding of the relationship between God and our world and ourselves. It allows us to share Christ's work of strengthening relationships of love within the world, and between the world and God.

Lessons from Elijah

Elijah the Tishbite, of Tishbe in Gilead, said to Ahab, 'As the LORD the God of Israel lives, before whom I stand, there shall be neither dew nor rain these years, except by my word.' The word of the LORD came to him, saying, 'Go from here and turn eastwards, and hide yourself by the Wadi Cherith, which is east of the Jordan. You shall drink from the wadi, and I have commanded the ravens to feed you there.' So he went and did according to the word of the LORD; he went and lived by the Wadi Cherith, which is east of the Jordan. The ravens brought him bread and meat in the morning, and bread and meat in the evening; and he drank from the wadi. But after a while the wadi dried up, because there was no rain in the land.

Then the word of the LORD came to him, saying, 'Go now to Zarephath, which belongs to Sidon, and live there, for I have commanded a widow there to feed you.' So he set out and went to Zarephath. When he came to the gate of the town, a widow was there gathering sticks; he called to her and said, 'Bring me a little water in a vessel, so that I may drink.' As she was going to bring it, he called to her and said, 'Bring me a morsel of bread in your hand.'

(1 Kings 17.1–11)

We often think of Old Testament prophets as being called to prophecy very suddenly and dramatically. In fact, when we look more closely, it isn't usually the case.

When we first meet Elijah in 1 Kings 17, he is already a prophet of some kind. The office of prophecy seems to have been an established part of the religious hierarchy of his day, so we should probably imagine him as a high-ranking religious professional, who acts as an adviser to King Ahab of Israel. We've no reason to suppose he was bad at his job, but the author of 1 Kings tell us nothing about it. He apparently thinks that until God told him to go into the desert, Elijah wasn't doing anything worth reporting. What is clear, though, is that Elijah's call didn't come out of the blue. It came after years of routine and committed, if perhaps less than inspired, service to God. (Elijah isn't the only prophet of whom this is true. Isaiah, for instance, was already a priest in the temple when he was called to prophecy.)

In one respect, the call of Elijah fulfils all the worst suspicions of the reluctant modern prophet. Before he can become the prophet we know, he has to learn a new perspective on society. From being a high-status and probably wealthy professional, he must become a beggar: homeless, helpless and completely dependent on the charity, first of God, and then of the lowest in society, a poor widow.

It is worth noticing the important part the widow plays in this story. When Elijah first asks her for food, she explains that she has not enough even to keep herself and her son alive. Elijah promises that if she shares what she has, the Lord won't let her provisions run out. The widow trusts him and risks taking him into her home. Together, the widow and Elijah learn an essential lesson: the meaning of neighbourliness. Though she is never named, the widow is a powerful figure: a model of faith and love. She reminds us how much religious leaders have to learn from the poor and disregarded. In this story, she gets her reward – not from Elijah, who has nothing, but from God, who enables Elijah to refill her flour and oil jars, and later to raise her son from the dead.

Elijah spends three years away from court, learning a lot about the uncertainty of life, and how dependent all human beings are on one another and on God. Then God tells him to go back and resume his career. Elijah is so successful in this new mission that he incurs the hatred of Queen Jezebel, who threatens to have him killed.

In terror, he flees into the desert, sits down under a broom tree, and suffers what looks like a major mid-life crisis. 'It is enough; now, O LORD, take away my life, for I am no better than my ancestors' (1 Kings 19.4). It is a revealing comment. Elijah has been not only successful, but ambitious. He wanted to be the best. He wanted to change the world. Now he's been reminded that he is only human.

God does not answer Elijah's complaint. He sends him deep into the desert, to Mount Horeb. Elijah drags himself up the mountain and takes shelter in a cave, still complaining.

> [God] said, 'Go out and stand on the mountain before the LORD, for the LORD is about to pass by.' Now there was a great wind, so strong that it was splitting mountains and breaking rocks in pieces before the LORD, but the LORD was not in the wind; and after the wind an earthquake, but the LORD was not in the earthquake; and after the earthquake a fire, but the LORD was not in the fire; and after the fire a sound of sheer silence. When Elijah heard it, he wrapped his face in his mantle and went out and stood at the entrance of the cave. Then there came a voice to him that said, 'What are you doing here, Elijah?'
> (I Kings 19.11–13)

Wind, fire, and earthquakes are all things which have signalled the presence of God in the past, but here, Elijah shows his greatest quality. In his darkest moment, he attends to God. He listens; he obeys; he intuits what does not, and what does signal the presence of God. He goes out to meet the silence, and listens again.

It is when Elijah commits himself, not to talking, but to listening – not to his own dreams and ambitions, but to God – that he is at his greatest as a prophet. God never does answer Elijah's complaints about his past life. Instead, he sends him on a new mission. And coming to his senses at last, and remembering perhaps that a prophet exists not to glorify himself but to serve God and his community, Elijah goes.

Elijah's prophetic career is a more dramatic one than most of us would want to contemplate. Even so, many of its themes are relevant to us. Elijah's ministry emerges from his existing way of life. It challenges him to expand his understanding of his society and its relationship with God. He has to learn to listen to God and to trust both God and other people, and it isn't always easy. But when he puts his trust in God, he overcomes every challenge and helps to transform his society.

Many calls, many missions

Next, the group turned to some more recent stories of prophecy closer to home.

Elizabeth Gurney (1780–1845) was born into a wealthy Quaker banking family and married another wealthy banker, Joseph Fry. When the family moved from London to rural Essex, Elizabeth, like many gentlewomen, did what she could to help the poor and sick of her village. She founded a school and established a winter soup-kitchen. These activities made her aware how poverty, debt, sickness or death caused many families to slip below the breadline. Some turned to crime to survive; some ended up on the streets, some in the workhouse. Unlike other gentlewomen, Elizabeth followed them there, visiting widows and the disabled and starting another school in the workhouse.

When the family moved back to London, Elizabeth visited Newgate prison, where women and children were then kept with little food or clothing and no heating, bedding or medical care. Shocked by what she found, she started a Quaker women's group to make baby clothes. She set up a school in the prison, and taught adult prisoners needlework so that they could earn a living when they were released.

Her activities prompted her to think about the prison system itself. She started to speak at public meetings, campaigning against the death penalty for minor offences. She investigated the convict ships which took women to Australia, found them as squalid as Newgate, and lobbied successfully for their improvement. Eventually, she became an adviser on prisons to local and national governments throughout Britain and all over Europe, arguing the importance of rehabilitation over punishment, and bringing about the end of a number of inhumane practices, such as chaining prisoners to walls.

Elizabeth Fry's prophetic greatness lies in the fact that, firmly rooted as she was in her class at a time when women were neither educated nor encouraged to think about much apart from marriage and a family, she could see beyond social divisions to the shared humanity of all the people she encountered. She did not experience a single call that changed her life. Her 'call' came in many small stages, but was no less powerful for that. She began by noticing how the people she tried to help suffered. She followed where their suffering took them, and took the further step of trying to help them. This path took her far from her social background and expectations, but she followed it faithfully. She was also very good at mustering support. She knew she couldn't make her reforms by herself, so she persuaded other people to help her.

Despite her remarkable success, Fry also felt that she had passed through times of great rejection, suffering and loneliness, and she compared herself explicitly with a prophet wandering in the wilderness. 'My life has been one of great vicissitude,' she wrote; 'mine has been a hidden path, hidden from every human eye. I have had deep humiliations and sorrows to pass through. I can truly say that I have "wandered in the wilderness in a solitary way, and found no city to dwell in"; and yet how wonderfully I have been sustained.'[1]

Not all prophets are called from a position of social privilege. Frederick Douglass was born in slavery in 1818, in the American state of Maryland. At the age of 20, he ran away and managed to work his way to New York. There he began to attend, and then to speak extempore at meetings of anti-slavery societies. Clever, handsome and a born orator, he made an immediate impact on the largely white, middle-class abolitionist movement.

Douglass's reputation grew steadily until in 1845, when he published his autobiography, he became an international celebrity. From then until his death in 1895, he wrote copiously, travelled all over the world to speak against slavery and racism, and worked for the political emancipation, education and economic development of American free blacks (as ex-slaves were known) and women.

Douglass understood how important it was for his cause to bridge the gulfs which existed between people of different races, birth and wealth, and he made sure he did it. This extract from a speech delivered in 1850 shows how skilfully he blended moving personal testimony with political argument and religious challenge:

The apologists for slavery often speak of the abuses of slavery; and they tell us that they are as much opposed to those abuses as we are; and that they would go as far to correct those abuses and to ameliorate the condition of the slave as anybody. The answer to that view is, that slavery is *itself* an abuse; that it lives by abuse; and dies by the absence of abuse. Grant that slavery is right; grant that the relation of master and slave may innocently exist; and there is not a single outrage which was ever committed against the slave but what finds an apology in the very necessity of the case. As was said by a slaveholder to the Methodist conference, 'If the relation be right, the means to maintain it are also right;' for without those means slavery could not exist. Remove the dreadful scourge – the plaited thong – the galling fetter – the accursed chain – and let the slaveholder rely solely upon moral and religious power, by which to secure obedience to his orders, and how long do you suppose a slave would remain on his plantation? The case only needs to be stated; it carries its own refutation with it.

Absolute and arbitrary power can never be maintained by one man over the body and soul of another man, without brutal chastisement and enormous cruelty.

To talk of *kindness* entering into a relation in which one party is robbed of wife, of children, of his hard earnings, of home, of friends, of society, of knowledge, and of all that makes this life desirable, is most absurd, wicked, and preposterous.[2]

Prophets have arisen in many different societies, but some qualities are common to them all. They all look beyond the values and assumptions of their own group, towards what is good for the whole community. They focus attention especially on the needs of those community members who are least able to speak or act for themselves. And they communicate effectively with those who have the power to change how society operates.

Some prophets accept or even welcome the title. Others reject it, like Amos, when King Jeroboam tells him to leave Israel and give up prophesying. 'I am no prophet,' Amos retorts (Amos 7.14–16), 'nor a prophet's son;' (he perhaps wants to distinguish his inspired warnings to Israel from the routine utterances of court prophets) 'but I am a herdsman, and a dresser of sycamore trees, and the LORD took me from following the flock, and the LORD said to me, "Go, prophesy to my people Israel." Now therefore hear the word of the LORD.' Whether he wanted the title or not, the writers of the Bible recognize Amos as a prophet, and we do the same with many modern men and women.

Prophecy now

No one in the Pentecost group had had the experience of trying to ignore a call to prophecy and being pursued by God as Jonah was. But several of us had had the experience of not doing something which we felt, deep down, we ought to do. We had felt a sense of guilt, and an obscure disappointment with ourselves that nibbled away at the back of our mind. We had become increasingly uncomfortable with ourselves. Some of our more forthright friends had asked why we seemed so twitchy and short-tempered. Quite often, like Jonah, we had eventually cracked, and done what we hadn't wanted to do – and then, even if it hadn't been easy, we had usually felt better.

Prophecy was definitely not one of the priestly ministries I felt drawn to before ordination. I aspired to become one of those peaceful, kindly, serene religious people. I dreamt of creating an environment of love and affirmation, never one of conflict and controversy. If I encountered unkindness or injustice, I hoped at the most to point it up with some barbless joke, the sort that would make everyone laugh and think at the same time.

It was a pity, in the circumstances, that my natural gifts ran to a critical eye, a short fuse and a sharp tongue. In my first few years as a priest, I may sometimes have managed kindness, but my attempts to become peaceful and serene were a complete and occasionally spectacular failure. Eventually, with a lot of regret and a little relief, I came to feel that some people just aren't cut out for serenity. But if so, then surely, I felt, there must be ways to use the qualities I did have in the service of God.

One thing a critical eye does allow one to do is to notice problems. Over the years, I had noticed a few in my workplace, which in the name of peacefulness I had tried to ignore. Now I started to face and speak up about unkindnesses or injustices I saw. Since I work in a liberal and humane institution in what in many ways is a progressive society, these were mostly small things, but they were things that mattered to the people who suffered them. Gradually, I found that the energy which generates anger in a person can also generate courage. The tongue which speaks one's own mind can speak equally well on behalf of other people.

The results were unexpectedly positive. It was a liberation to feel that I could and should speak up about things I felt were wrong. Even better, I often found more support among my colleagues than I'd expected. A lot of people, it turned out, had noticed the same things and were unhappy about them, but didn't have the temperament to make a fuss. Given a bit of cover by someone more outspoken, they were ready to acknowledge and try to solve all kinds of problems.

We all, I concluded, have different gifts, and most, if not all those gifts can be used prophetically. It's just a matter of working out how.

Some prophetic ministries develop as an indirect, rather than direct result of experience. Sheila Cassidy grew up as a Roman Catholic and more than once tested her vocation for religious life, but her principal life's work unfolded from a different and unexpected direction. As a young doctor, she worked in General Pinochet's Chile, and while there, she was imprisoned and tortured for treating a wounded revolutionary. After her release, she became an outspoken advocate of human rights. Later, her experience of suffering also contributed to her becoming one of the pioneers of the hospice movement in Britain. She has written extensively about the importance of integrating spirituality and secular work, and describes her work for the hospice movement as a prophetic ministry.

I have become aware that the hospice has come to stand in prophetic relationship to the mainstream of medical care in our area . . .

[Hospices] are able to carry out this prophetic function because they fulfil three major criteria: they are drawn from the mainstream of society to live and work at one remove from it; they have the contemplative space to reflect on the problems confronting them; and they do not choose this role but find themselves speaking a truth that they cannot contain . . .

Prophets . . . are individuals or groups of people who are called both to *listen* and to *speak out*. They must listen to God, to the 'signs of the times' and to the cries of the oppressed and when they have understood the message, speak out, what-ever the personal cost. Prophets are no holier than anyone else. They are frequently very wounded people – but like Jeremiah or Isaiah, they put their woundedness at the service of God. When they hear the voice which says, 'Whom shall I send? Who will be our messenger?' to their horror, they find themselves answering, 'Here I am; send me!' (Isaiah 6.8) . . .

The fact is that prophetic messages are, almost by definition, unwelcome because they challenge the accepted status quo . . . Amnesty International shouts its truth about imprisonment and torture from the housetops and persists in writing impor-tunate letters to busy politicians and dictators. Greenpeace gets its silly rainbow boats in the way of important nuclear tests and the anti-smoking lobby keeps drawing attention to the five billion pound revenue the government receives from cigarette advertising. It is the same in the medical world. Just when the government is trying to tidy up the shambolic National Health Service and make it more efficient, health workers *will* go on about the emotional needs of the sick and ask for more resources for such tedious and unproductive groups as the elderly, the handicapped and the dying.[3]

We think of prophets most often as critics of their societies: people who see something that needs to change, and speak and act to try to change it. But not all prophets are prophets of doom or injustice. We have already mentioned Anna, who recognizes the baby Jesus in the Temple as the redeemer of Jerusalem (Luke 2.36–8), and speaks out to thank God for a great blessing. Sometimes the role of a prophet is simply to remind people to be happy and to enjoy God's creation. Here is the poet Thomas Traherne (1637–74), in his *Centuries of Meditations*, doing just that:

Can you be Holy without accomplishing the end for which you are created? Can you be Divine unless you be Holy? Can you accomplish the end for which you were created, unless you be Righteous? Can you then be Righteous, unless you be just in rendering to Things their due esteem? All things were made to be yours, and you were made to prize them according to their value: which is your office and duty, the end for which you were created, and the means whereby you enjoy. The end for which you were created, is that by prizing all that God hath done, you may enjoy yourself and Him in Blessedness.[4]

Prophetic calls may come out of years of religious service, or none. They may come to the privileged or to the oppressed. They may come directly out of people's experience, or indirectly; suddenly and clearly, or stealthily, over time. They may be welcome or unwelcome. Some prophets are critical of their world, while others see good things that others do not see. Some prophets are heard, understood, and honoured; others are ignored, misunderstood and reviled. But all prophets both learn from their communities and serve them. They all learn by looking and listening attentively to the world, and they continue to look and listen as well as speak out. They all learn to stand to some extent both within and outside their society. And they all, first and last, trust God, serve God, and put their lives and ministry in God's hands.

When our Pentecost group had read and reflected on these examples, we agreed that even if we weren't very keen to be prophets now, it was an important strand in Christian tradition. For anyone who is trying to live a life of faith, it is worth being open to the possibility that we may be called at some point to prophetic ministry.

Prophecy – local and global

But if we were going to take seriously the possibility that one day we might feel called to any kind of prophetic activity, our group felt that we needed a better idea of what kind of prophecy would be possible in our own, immediate society – our villages of Sandford and Littlemore. So we began to think about what people had been doing locally in recent years. We soon realized that quite a number of individuals and groups could be described as acting prophetically. Starting with situations and activities they were already involved in, they had spotted a problem or a need, worked out a way to meet it, and put their plan into practice. In the process, they had strengthened the whole community.

The oldest religious building still in use in Littlemore is the Baptist chapel, which was established in the early nineteenth century. The current congregation is small, but it has a strong sense of mission. A few years ago, the members decided to explore new ways in which the chapel building itself, which is quite large, could be used to communicate the gospel. They prayed and discussed at length what the greatest needs of the area were, and concluded that one of our most serious problems is homelessness. Working with the local council and the housing department, they converted the chapel into housing for around 15 formerly home-less people. They continue to use the building's communal space for weekly worship.

Charlene's mission came to her when she realized how many elderly and housebound people in the area have no close fam-ily or more mobile friends to visit them regularly. Recruiting the local clergy and council services to help her, she set up a scheme through which people volunteer to visit one or two of their neigh-bours regularly, shop for them if necessary and pick up medical prescriptions.

Margreet, the vicar of Littlemore parish church, and her husband Julian were worried about the number of people who, not by choice, found themselves alone at Christmas, so they founded the community Christmas lunch. Now in its eighth year, it brings together 60 people or more to share Christmas day in the local primary school hall, and it has gained such a reputation that whole families now choose to join in rather than celebrating Christmas at home.

All these projects arose in different ways from prophetic visions. They began when someone saw that our small society was, in one way or another, not working as well, as lovingly, as it might. They all worked and continue to work because they answer a real need effectively, and also because they are enjoyable and fruitful in themselves. They have become places where people grow in respect and love for one another. None of them has an explicitly religious agenda, but they are all great examples of mission through ministry.

It is possible, we concluded, as an individual or a small group, to make a major impact on a specific issue in a small community. But some of the group also pointed out that we can all also act prophetically on bigger issues in the wider community.

Two of the greatest problems facing today's world as a whole are inequalities of wealth and power, within and between nations, and damage to the environment. Most of us will not be directly involved in leading large-scale, international, governmental or non-governmental initiatives to reduce inequalities of wealth and power, or to protect and clean up the environment. But we can all contribute to those initiatives in our everyday lives. When we buy fairly traded food and resist buying cheap clothes that have been made in sweatshops; when we cycle to work or take a train instead of the car; when we give a portion of what we earn to charities or turn down the central heating – we are taking part in an act of prophetic witness.

When the Make Poverty History campaign was launched in Britain in 2005, churches all over the country took a particular interest in it. They advertised it, preached about it and organized numerous local events to raise funds for it. In-house research by the Department for International Development and a group of charities working in overseas aid found that Christian individuals and churches did more than any other group to spread news and information about the campaign. Their prophetic work and witness was crucial in making the campaign the success it has been.

This chapter began by suggesting that prophecy is a form of love, and earlier we saw that at the heart of love stands the recognition that we are one body: one human race; one creation. In the globally networked and interwoven economies, societies and cultures of the twenty-first century, it is easy to see more and more ways in which the whole human race is one. Thanks to science, it is also becoming ever clearer how we are one with the rest of the material world.

There have always been stories about the unity of creation – in the book of Genesis, God creates humanity out of the same clay as other living things – but modern science has shown it to us as physical fact. We have learned that the particles and energies which make us who we are, are the same particles and energies that make everything else. We know that they have been used countless times before in other materials and beings, and will be recycled countless times again. We have established that we share nearly all our DNA with other primates, most of it with other mammals and some of it with practically every living thing. We are, not only spiritually and metaphorically, but in the most practical and material ways, one body: one with each other and with the whole universe.

Some theologians have used these discoveries to reflect in new ways on the relationship between the physical world and the divine. In Christian tradition, our physical bodies have often been regarded as at best irrelevant to our spiritual life, and at worst a dangerous source of spiritually damaging temptation. Nowadays, we are more likely to be taught that our bodies as well as our hearts, minds and spirits are part of God's gift to us and our gift back to God.

Sallie McFague goes further still and suggests that the whole of creation is one with God – one body created out of Godself and remaining always part of the divine. In this passage from *The Body of God: An Ecological Theology*, she reflects on the importance of the fact that we are beings materially continuous with the rest of creation, and its implications for our spiritual unity with one another and with God:

We ought to love and honour the body, our own bodies, and the bodies of all the other life-forms on the planet. The body is not a discardable garment cloaking the real self or essence of a person (or a pine tree or a chimpanzee); rather, it is the shape and form of who we are. It is how each of us is recognized, responded to, loved, touched, and cared for – as well as oppressed, beaten, raped, mutilated, discarded and killed. The body is not a minor matter . . .

Most of us live with the strange illusion that we are other than our bodies. Centuries of Christian speculation about life after death have encouraged a diffidence toward the body at best, distrust and hatred of it at worst. That attitude is at the heart of one of the central crises of our time: the inability to love the 'body' of the earth. The ecological crisis will not begin to turn around until we change at a very basic level how we feel about bodies and about the material creation in all its incredible variety and richness of forms. It is not enough to change our life-styles; we must change what we value. We must come to value bodies, to love them, and appreciate each of them in their differences from us and from each other. The body of the earth, teeming with variety, is but a tiny cell in the 'body' of the universe, which includes all matter in all its forms over 15 billion years of evolutionary history.

But let us press this model one step further . . . If we and everything else that exists in the universe are matter, are body, then can we also speak of 'the body of God'? In fact, must we not do so?

In this body model, God would not be transcendent over the universe in the sense of external or apart from it, but would be the source, power and goal – the spirit – that enlivens (and loves) the entire process and its material forms. As we are inspirited bodies – living, loving, thinking bodies – so, imagining God in our own image (and how else *can* we model God?), we speak of God as the inspirited body of the entire universe, the animating, living spirit that produces, guides, and saves all that is.[5]

When we see ourselves as materially continuous with the rest of creation, and all creation as part of God, then it is impossible to avoid the conclusion that by damaging any part of creation we are damaging ourselves and acting against God. It's hard to imagine a stronger prophetic witness to the importance of looking after the world we live in. It calls us all to do everything we can to care for all living things and every part of our environment, to help sustain and enrich both human and non-human life for the future.

Prophecy and social action

As our discussion about prophecy developed, the Pentecost group realized that it was increasingly becoming a discussion about social action. We shouldn't have been surprised: when we try, not just to identify problems in our society but to do something about them, then prophecy and social action are inevitably intertwined. This has always been true: many prophets of the past have worked tirelessly for the social change for which they have called. It is also appropriate, since to live as a Christian means to love God and one's neighbour with all one's heart, soul, mind *and* strength. It would be wrong to feel that something was wrong and not to speak out; it would be wrong to speak and not to act.

Different people see and are stirred by different problems – local, national and global. But the Pentecost group came to see the message of the gospel as a challenge to respond when we feel stirred: to do more than talk back to the television, or grumble to our neighbours, or let ourselves feel oppressed by the imperfections of the world. We are all in a position to do something, and no word, no action, is too small to make a difference.

Questions for discussion

- What gifts do you have which might have prophetic uses?
- Where in the places where you live or work might there be a need for prophetic speech or action?
- What could you do?

4

Forgiveness and reconciliation

Forgiveness and reconciliation: the heart of the good news

If, to members of the Pentecost discussion group, prophecy at first seemed very different from listening, forgiveness and reconciliation at first seemed very different from prophecy. Prophets are challenging and sometimes controversial figures. They speak out and work for change, and in the process they often have to overcome opposition. On the face of it, nothing could be further from the practice of forgiveness and reconciliation.

We had also seen, though, that many prophets act to right wrongs, and help to heal divisions in their societies. This suggests that prophecy and reconciliation – seeing a problem and working to resolve it – might be more closely entwined than we had thought. Both might be expressions of love. Either way, we all agreed that forgiveness and reconciliation are central to Christianity, so they must form one of the most important parts of any Christian's daily ministry.

The heart of the gospel, as it has been preached since the first Pentecost, is that Jesus Christ, by his death and resurrection, overcame humanity's long self-estrangement from God, and made it possible for us to turn and be reunited in God's loving embrace.

By always loving God and his fellow human beings, by refusing to respond to hostility with hostility, and by forgiving even those who betrayed and crucified him, Christ acted as a kind of firebreak to evil: an impenetrable barrier, someone in whom it could not work and through whom it could not spread. Instead, he radiated the love of God, which spread from him to everyone who came into contact with him with an open heart.

As Christians, one of the principal ways we follow Christ is by making sure that, if humanly possible, evil does not breed in and around us. The Pentecost group looked at two ways of doing this: by defusing the negative qualities within ourselves that block the action of God's Spirit through us, and, first, by practising forgiveness and reconciliation.

From prophecy to forgiveness and reconciliation

The Old Testament tells several stories of characters whose activities have a prophetic dimension, but who are honoured for the gentleness and constructiveness of their approach to social problems. The Pentecost group chose to look at the story of Esther.

The book of Esther is set in the early fifth century BC. Israel is under Persian rule. Esther and her foster-father Mordecai live in Babylon – one of the many Israelite families who have made lives outside Israel and careers in the service of the Persian kings.

Esther, who is very beautiful, attracts the attention of the Persian king Ahasuerus. He makes her his queen, not realizing that she is Jewish. Soon afterwards, Mordecai, who is a court official, falls foul of another official, Haman. Haman tells the king that the Jews living in his empire prefer their own laws to those of the kingdom. He advises that they should be rooted out. The king agrees, and orders that all the Jews in the empire shall be killed. When Mordecai hears the news, he goes to Esther and begs her to use her position to get the edict revoked.

Esther is terrified. If the king discovers she is Jewish, she will be killed. At first she refuses to help, but Mordecai doesn't give up, and eventually Esther promises to approach the king. She does so with skill and diplomacy. For two nights, she dresses in her finest robes and entertains the king with lavish banquets. Highly gratified, the king promises to grant her any request. Esther begs for the lives of herself and her people.

The king is moved by her beauty and enraged by Haman's trickery. He cancels his edict, has Haman executed, promotes Mordecai, and publishes another edict praising the Jews for their loyalty to himself and the justice of their laws. The story ends with the Jews becoming honoured members of Persian society, many Persians converting to Judaism, and Esther, Mordecai and the king living happily ever after.

The Book of Esther is a mixture of history, court story and fable, but the point it makes is profound. By finding the courage to tell the Persian king that his attitude to the Jews was unjust, Esther brought about a radical change in Persian society. By a combination of political skill, prophetic outspokenness and reconciliation, she transformed the situation of her community.

In the New Testament, when relationships within the earliest Christian communities are being discussed, prophecy, forgiveness and reconciliation often go together. Those who write with advice to communities about how to live, recognize that problems will develop and people will make mistakes and fall out. It is important both that mistakes are recognized and pointed out, and that the community has ways of addressing them, achieving reconciliation and moving on.

The apostle Paul tells the Galatians (6.1–5) that if someone is caught transgressing, he or she should be corrected, but gently, and the correctors should look to their own consciences at the same time. The author of the Letter to the Ephesians tells the Ephesians to speak the truth to each other – even to get angry – but not to let the sun set on their anger. If they must criticize each other, they should do it with kindness and compassion, and without bitterness, anger, malice or slander (4.25–32).

In Matthew's Gospel (18.15–22), Jesus gives the disciples a set of instructions for addressing and solving problems in future communities of faith:

'If another member of the church sins against you, go and point out the fault when the two of you are alone. If the member listens to you, you have regained that one. But if

you are not listened to, take one or two others along with
you, so that every word may be confirmed by the evidence
of two or three witnesses. If the member refuses to listen to
them, tell it to the church; and if the offender refuses to
listen even to the church, let such a one be to you as a Gentile
and a tax-collector ...' Then Peter came and said to him,
'Lord, if another member of the church sins against me, how
often should I forgive? As many as seven times?' Jesus said to
him, 'Not seven times, but, I tell you, seventy-seven times.'
(Matt. 18.15–17, 21–22)

These instructions address mistakes by individuals rather than
groups of people, but their approach could work with either. You
begin by trying to solve a problem privately. If that doesn't work,
you go public by steps. If the worst comes to the worst, you treat the
problematic person (or group) 'like a Gentile and a tax-collector'.

That last phrase is often taken to mean that wrongdoers are
thrown out of the community, which has nothing more to do with
them. Its context in Matthew's Gospel, though, suggests a different
interpretation.

One of Jesus' disciples was a tax collector, and a number of
Gentiles become followers of Jesus. Jesus himself says that he comes
'to call not the righteous but sinners' (9.13). And it is in Matthew's
Gospel that Jesus calls his followers to love, not just their neighbours, but their enemies too (5.45–48). That being so, Gentiles
and tax collectors are not so much people that followers of
Christ have nothing to do with, as people who simply are not (or
not yet) members of the community. So even if the Christian
community excludes a troublemaker, by regarding him or her as
a Gentile or a tax collector, it leaves the door open for that person
to come back in again at some point in the future. Love does not
despair of anyone.

Making and keeping peace within a community is a many-
sided activity. It helps if we understand the people around us – why
they are as they are and behave as they do. To do that, we must
practise attentiveness towards them, and be good neighbours over

time. We also need to be honest about why we are as we are and behave as we do, both to ourselves and each other. And it helps if all sides are able to express their views clearly but calmly, without letting anger, resentment or offence cloud the issue.

Some members of the group pointed out that all this takes a lot of practice, and since we are all imperfect human beings, we may not find it easy to make and maintain loving relationships with other members of our community. We agreed to come back to that discussion in a later week. Meanwhile, though, we also agreed that however much we practised, we probably weren't going to become perfect in this life. So living in peace would also mean being prepared to compromise and to accept that sometimes we have to agree to disagree and find ways to live with it.

Repentance and forgiveness

We hadn't been talking about forgiveness long before we hit a fundamental and very difficult question. Should we forgive everyone, or only people who have recognized what they have done wrong, said sorry and asked forgiveness for it?

One or two members of the group thought this was not a difficult question at all. The Gospels agree that before Jesus began his ministry, John the Baptist appeared in the wilderness by the river Jordon, calling the people of Israel to repent of their sins and prepare themselves to meet the Messiah. When Jesus begins his ministry, the essence of his proclamation is: 'The time is fulfilled, and the kingdom of God has come near; repent, and believe in [or 'trust'] the good news' (Mark 1.15). Whether repenting comes before believing, or whether they come together, it seems clear that both come before God's forgiveness.

Next we looked at one of Jesus' healing miracles, where healing seems to be an expression of forgiveness, after people have put their faith in Jesus. A paralytic is brought to Jesus by a group of friends who are convinced that Jesus can heal him (Matt. 9.1–7). Jesus sees their faith, and says, 'Take heart, son; your sins are forgiven.' The man picks up his bed and walks. One member of the group pointed out that faith comes before healing in other stories too. When, for instance, the woman with the haemorrhage touches Jesus' cloak in the hope of being cured (Matt. 9.18–22), Jesus says to her, 'Take heart, daughter; your faith has made you well.'

We noticed that in both these stories, Jesus tells the person who is healed to 'take heart', *tharsein* in Greek. *tharsein* can also mean 'have courage', 'have confidence', 'have faith', or 'do not be afraid'. Faith, confidence and not being afraid are themes which are central to the whole New Testament, so we should probably hear something of all those meanings here. If so, Jesus seems to be telling people to *have* faith when they have shown faith already. It reminded us of the strange prayer of the man whose son's demon is cast out by Jesus: 'I believe; help my unbelief!'[1]

But when Jesus tells people who have already shown faith in him, to *have* faith, he hints that faith is not necessarily something we get all at once. It may be something which grows gradually and deepens over time. If that is so, then perhaps repentance is also something which does not always happen once and for all, but which grows and develops in us gradually.

In all sorts of ways, we agreed, experience suggests that this is often what happens.

I remember when I first began to understand the complicated relationship between suffering, repentance, healing and forgiveness. I was on holiday in Malta, my first holiday for a year. I was exhausted, stressed and resentful that I'd had to work through the previous few months without a break. I had also recently broken up with a boyfriend, and I was still angry about the split.

Ministering in a parish had made me feel that one of the most important things any human being can do for another is to act as a channel of God's love. I wanted to bring peace and the assurance of God's healing to the people with whom I lived and worked. In the previous few months I had begun to feel I couldn't do it. I was too stressed, too angry inside. I was afraid that, one day, someone would say or do something just slightly wrong, and I would crack and lash out at them unforgivably.

One afternoon, I knelt in the little Maltese church which com-
memorates the shipwreck of St Paul and said, 'Lord, I'm in a mess.
I can't deal with it alone. *Please* help.' It was a moment of deep
repentance and desperate faith.

There was no vision; no miraculous cure. But over the next few
days, I had a sense of being held – firmly, like a screaming baby.
Through my distress, I dimly realized that although I was hurting,
I wasn't abandoned. Eventually, like a baby, I began to calm down.
I felt safe. More than that, I felt loved. Beneath all the stress and
suffering was something solid; a place of rest. I let myself slump
there, exhausted, grateful to let go of my troubles for a while. The
sense of being safe, of being loved, did not change. It was all right.
Fundamentally, everything was all right.

Eventually, I began to sit up and take an interest in the world
again. And then I realized that rock bottom is well named. In the
depths of my misery and confusion, I had hit something solid: an
experience of love – immoveable, unbreakable, unconditional. It
was not just an endpoint, but a beginning. A foundation. Something
on which one might begin to build life again; a life perhaps more
whole, less damaged than the last one. Maybe, just maybe, building on that foundation, I would be able to smile again. I would
be able to reach out, smiling, to other people.

That experience of rock bottom became for me an experience
of divine love, of forgiving and healing grace, which were there
long before I crashed into them in my misery.

The crisis passed – the holiday ended. The sense of standing on
a solid foundation stayed with me. I began tentatively to rebuild.
I accepted the end of my relationship. I resolved not to hang
on to suffering in the future until it turned bad inside me and
started to infect other people.

So far, so good; but I was not fully healed. We rarely are, after
just one crisis. Other members of the group had had similar
experiences of suffering which had reached a crisis and at least a
partial resolution. We all agreed that the greater the suffering and
our need for healing and forgiveness, the longer the process tends
to be.

It takes time to mend a damaged heart and mind. Often we tick over for a while, feeling better, hopeful of feeling better still. Then perhaps we start to slide back into our old ways of feeling, thinking and acting, or perhaps another trauma throws us into another crisis and another degree of healing. And so it goes on, for most of us: periods of repentance and amendment alternating with periods of stagnation or backsliding.

But just as most of us don't repent once, for all our brokenness, so we should perhaps think of forgiveness as coming to us bit by bit. In the Catholic practice of confession, we repent of specific failings and are absolved of them, and we can go to confession as often as we need to. Many liturgies begin with a communal prayer of repentance for our sins of thought, word and deed, and the promise that our sins will be forgiven. We may have a good idea that later the same day, or the next day, or the next week, we will come back, still damaged and imperfect beings, and have to repent again, but we are never refused forgiveness.

Like a broken leg or a damaged organ, damaged and imperfect humanity takes time to heal, even when we're doing everything we can to help ourselves. The forgiveness we are given every time we ask for it, heals us a little more and encourages us to keep doing what we can to avoid doing more damage to ourselves and others.

Forgiveness before everything

There is another strand in Christian teaching about forgiveness, which puts forgiveness at the very beginning of the process of reconciliation between God and humanity. In St Luke's Gospel (23.34), Jesus becomes the model for this kind of forgiveness when he says of the people who are crucifying him, 'Father, forgive them; for they do not know what they are doing.'[2] St Paul also explores it in his Letter to the Romans:

God proves his love for us in that while we still were sinners Christ died for us. Much more surely then, now that we have been justified [made righteous] by his blood, will we be saved

through him from the wrath of God. For if while we were
enemies, we were reconciled to God through the death of his
Son, much more surely, having been reconciled, will we be
saved by his life.   (Rom. 5.8–10)

Paul expresses his confidence that God has already forgiven humanity for their sins before humanity has done anything at all. God
sends Christ to die for us, because God knows that we are not
capable on our own of the kind of repentance and change of
life that we need to reconcile us with God. Christ's self-sacrifice
for us on the cross is in some sense an act of repentance on our
behalf. It reconciles us with God, even before we respond to the
good news that God's kingdom is at hand.

It is probably this idea, that forgiveness precedes repentance,
which is behind the difficult question so often asked by radio and
television interviewers of Christians who have suffered any kind
of wrong: 'Do you forgive the person who did this to you?' The
trouble with this question is that if the interviewee says 'Yes', then
Christian forgiveness can sound like a kind of 'Get out of gaol
free' card – suggesting that whatever anyone else does, a Christian
will always forgive. If the interviewee says 'No', he or she is in
danger of sounding courageous but uncharitable. The interviewee,
unfortunately, rarely gets time to explain how he or she really
understands forgiveness.

Christian forgiveness is never a 'Get out of gaol free' card. It
never says that whatever anyone does is OK because God forgives
us all, and we too ought to forgive everybody everything.

One way to understand what Paul says about God's forgiveness
is to see it as God's making reconciliation *available*, rather than,
as it were, a done deal. We may be forgiven – that is an attitude
in the heart of God – but for forgiveness to be made practical,
for us to be reconciled, we have to turn to God and ask for it.
And Christians may imitate God and Christ by trying to develop
a forgiving heart – a heart which tries to understand and to love
someone who does wrong – but for that forgiveness to turn into
active reconciliation, the other person must ask for it.

This understanding of Christian forgiveness is widely held. Several members of the Pentecost group held it. But others felt strongly that it could not be the whole story.

We had agreed that a large part of who and what we are is the result of our past relationships. We all help to make each other the people we are today. This means that when people behave in destructive ways, towards themselves or others, it is often because they have been hurt or damaged in the past.

People who are greedy, for instance, whether for food, love, attention or material goods, often want those things because they feel starved of them. People may behave aggressively because they have been hurt before, and are afraid of being hurt again. People who treat their loved ones badly may be trying to make up for being abused or abandoned themselves. If we have had a bad experience very young, or repeatedly over time, or at a specially impressionable moment in our lives, the damage can be deep and far-reaching.

We agreed that this kind of hurt is hard to grow out of. It's especially hard to grow out of by ourselves, even if we want to. So we need to take this into account when we are thinking about whether and how to forgive one another.

If someone is badly damaged by terrible experiences, it probably won't be enough to tell that person that we'll be reconciled when he or she has repented and changed. Change may simply not be possible without help and encouragement – and not just a word of encouragement once, but consistent help, over time. But if we are willing to help and encourage someone, then to some extent we have already forgiven that person. We are already, at least partially, reconciled, and are taking him or her into our love.

If most of us are to change, to grow out of the damage that has become ingrained in us and shaped our growing, to be healed of the harm which we do to ourselves and others, then we need space and time to do it. We need people around us who react to our words and behaviour not with fear, disapproval or aggression, confirming our negative view of the world, but with love, confidence and an affirmation that we can learn to feel, think and act differently. We need a model, a vision of what we're aiming for. All these are much more powerful incentives to change than just being told that if we change first, then we'll be forgiven. If we hope to become as loving and loveable as we can be, then we all need an environment of love, trust and hope in which to do it.

That environment, the group agreed, ideally needs to be not only spiritual, but physical. We need the help, not only of God, Christ and the Holy Spirit, but of each other. One of the most important things we can do, as followers of Christ, is to create a place of reconciliation for one another – to encourage each other towards healing, growth and forgiveness.

Forgiveness and reconciliation in the Lord's Prayer and after

The next question that challenged the Pentecost group was: As Christians, do we have a choice whether we forgive people or not? To help us think about this question, we looked at how people have interpreted one small but crucial word in the New Testament.

In Matthew's version of the Lord's Prayer (6.9–13), Jesus teaches his disciples to pray, 'Forgive us our debts [or 'sins'], as we also have forgiven our debtors.' The little word 'as' (as short in Greek as in English) makes a powerful link between God's forgiveness of us and our forgiveness of each other. Early commentators, however, disagreed about what exactly the link meant.

Tertullian, writing around the end of the second century, quotes St Luke (6.37): 'Forgive, and you will be forgiven', and says that we must forgive each other before we can even hope for God's forgiveness. Cyprian, not much later, agrees, but stresses that our forgiveness of each other comes out of our sense that we need to be forgiven by God.[3]

Origen, writing in the third century, takes a slightly different view. He points out that we are all, in practice, debtors in hundreds of ways: to our families, friends and community, and above all to

God. Many of these debts are good and joyful ones – like the debts we owe our family and friends for loving us – and the appropriate response is not to try to get rid of the debt, but to make the most of the relationship. The same is true with God. God creates and forms us. Christ buys our freedom from slavery to sin with his blood. The Holy Spirit marks us out for redemption. The response should be to love God as God loves us.

We could never repay our debts to God, or family or friends, even if we wanted to. And we *want* to stay connected by interlocking debts of love. But sometimes we get into debt in the wrong way, when we have abused our relationship with God or each other. Then we owe God or the other person a heartfelt apology and perhaps practical reparation too.

When someone gets into our debt in the wrong way, Origen says, we remember all the good debts we share: all the ways we belong together, as part of the same creation and shared communities. We don't want to lose that good indebtedness, so we try to be tolerant of each other's weaknesses and wrongdoings. We also remember that we aren't perfect ourselves, and we don't want our own imperfections to destroy all the good in our relationships. So we shouldn't make our mistakes and wrongdoings a reason to sever relationships, but do what we can to help each other turn our lives around. In the same way, we hope and believe that God will never end God's relationship with us because of our mistakes and wrongdoings, but rather help us to change our hearts and our behaviour, and repair our relationship.

Ultimately, for Origen, we forgive each other because we already trust that through Christ, God forgives us, and because our relationships on earth should be a model of God's loving relationship with us all.[4] We shall return to this idea in Chapter 5, but here the important point is what all the early commentators on the Lord's Prayer agree on. Forgiveness and reconciliation are not optional for Christians. They stand at the very heart of what it means to follow Christ, and to love God and our neighbours.

Can we all learn to repent and be healed by being forgiven by those around us? We can't be sure, but in recent years, some remarkable experiments in political forgiveness and reconciliation have been made, which offer strong grounds for hope.

A number of countries around the world have marked radical changes of political direction with a brave determination by all parties to face up to the crimes which individuals and groups have previously committed. Commissions have been established, before which people can come to confess their wrongdoings and ask for forgiveness of those whom they have hurt. In each case, the turmoil which the country has previously suffered has been prolonged, violent and incalculably damaging to all involved. Large numbers of individuals have been involved in every kind of abuse and violation of their neighbours. Reconciliation has depended on people finding a willingness in themselves to forgive one another, even before repentance has been expressed, and to create a space in which repentance, change and growth can happen.

The most famous example of this process is the Truth and Reconciliation Commission which was established in South Africa after the political revolution which brought an end to apartheid. Desmond Tutu, Archbishop of Cape Town and Chairman of the Commission, described the work of the commission like this:

> Here the central concern is not retribution or punishment but, in the spirit of *ubuntu* [roughly translatable as 'humane-ness', the distinctively human quality of gentleness and compassion], the healing of breaches, the redressing of imbalances, the restoration of broken relationships. This kind of justice seeks to rehabilitate both the victim and the perpetrator, who should be given the opportunity to be reintegrated into the community he or she has injured by his or her offence.[5]

People who appeared in front of the Commission apologized and asked forgiveness for their crimes, gained immunity from prosecution. Those who took part expressed no doubt that, although the reconciliation process was inevitably not universal or perfect, far more was achieved to bring peace and healing among South Africans by this means than could possibly have been achieved by trying to prosecute all those, on all sides, who had committed crimes against other South Africans during the era of apartheid. Though not all those who took part in the process were Christians, Archbishop Tutu explicitly characterized it as inspired by the Christian understanding of forgiveness.

Organizations which work for forgiveness and reconciliation do not need to be founded by governments to be effective and influential. In Northern Ireland, a number of such groups arose within the community at the height of the troubles of the late twentieth century. Some, like the Corrymeela Community, have an explicitly Christian inspiration; others, like the Peace and Reconciliation Group (PRG), do not; but all work with a wide range of both individuals and groups to heal the religious, political and cultural divisions which have ravaged Irish society. On its website, the Corrymeela Community describes its mission like this:

> Founded in 1965, Corrymeela's objective has always been and continues to be promoting reconciliation and peace-building through the healing of social, religious and political divisions in Northern Ireland. Corrymeela's history is built upon committed work with individuals and communities which have suffered through the violence and polarisation of the Northern Irish conflict. Our vision of Christian community and reconciliation has been expressed through a commitment of promoting interaction between and building positive relationships among all kinds and conditions of people.

The Peace and Reconciliation Group explain on their website that:

> A major strand of our work involves getting people to talk to one another. This may happen in the form of structured workshops or training programmes, specifically designed projects, mediation sessions, or in a more private way, as our organisation is known as an unbiased, impartial group and can provide a neutral space for people to meet or seek refuge if necessary.

Like the Truth and Reconciliation Commission, Corrymeela and PRG are frequently asked to share their experience and expertise, working with divided communities all over the world.

It is a lot to ask of one person or one community which has been injured by another, that they offer forgiveness and the opportunity of reconciliation. It doesn't get any easier when two or more people or communities have hurt each other. Initiatives like the Truth and Reconciliation Commission, Corrymeela and PRG don't ask any one group or participant to do all the forgiving. They recognize that in the situations they work in, people on all sides have both done and suffered damage. They try to encourage everyone both to recognize and ask forgiveness for the damage they have inflicted, and to try to forgive the damage that has been done to them.

When the process works, all sides move gradually, simultaneously, towards listening to each other, trusting each other and ultimately being reconciled with each other. The same is often true in less extreme situations and relationships. It may be more helpful not to think of one person offering all the forgiveness and opportunity for reconciliation in a difficult situation, but of everyone concerned learning both to offer and accept forgiveness and reconciliation at the same time. Having said that, one person may still often have to make the first move.

Some members of the group commented that there are people so damaged that they have no healing to offer anyone else, and it takes an exceptional person or group to offer an environment in which they could be healed. Others pointed out that there are also people so damaged that it would take more than a lifetime to undo all their damage and enable them to flourish in love. But we thought that most of us, suffering from the ordinary crop of failings which afflict most people, could perhaps hope to help each other, step by step, to change our lives by the practice of pre-emptive forgiveness and reconciliation.

Indirect forgiveness

Another difficulty with forgiveness also occurred to the group. Given that we are all imperfect beings, and most of us are hurt and warped in one way or another, it may not always be possible for the person who has been hurt by another to be the person who forgives them and enables them to be reconciled. We all agreed that it is a misuse of the idea of forgiveness – and a depressingly common one – if, for instance, someone tells a battered wife that she should forgive her husband and stick by him, or an abused child that he should forgive his abuser. Sometimes, the experiences and situations of the people involved may mean that it is better for them to get right away from one another. Or sometimes, people who might have been able to achieve reconciliation are parted by circumstances – by one person's moving away, or falling ill, or dying.

In these situations, I suggested, the wider community has a vital role to play. If one person who has been harmed by another is not in a position to offer love and reconciliation, then someone else in the community, or the community as a whole, may be able to take up the case.

It is important to remember that in this situation, the community isn't by any means giving the offender a 'Get out of gaol free' card. It is acting as a representative of the damaged person, to give the offender a space in which to grow and change. In such a situation we may, as Christ did, help to forgive – to bring to reconciliation and transformation – people who have not hurt us, but have hurt others.

The person who taught me this lesson was a friend who came from a family which had been traumatized over generations by poverty, crime, imprisonment and domestic violence. My friend (whom I'll call Jane) seemed, at first sight, to have escaped her unhappy past. By the time I knew her, she was happily married, with a loving husband who had a secure job, her own home, and children who were thriving. But she bore the scars of her family's history. They came out in insecurity, depression and anger, in occasionally violent verbal attacks on the people closest to her, and she did not seem to know how to heal the pain that obviously festered inside her.

Jane's family suffered too from her suffering, and some of them found it hard to deal with. I, being less close to her, found her outbursts less traumatic. At the same time, it was easy to see her many wonderful qualities. She was a devoted wife and mother, a wonderful cook, a loyal friend and a tirelessly caring neighbour. She contributed to her local community in a hundred ways. Despite working extremely hard, she found time to be creative, hospitable and profoundly attentive to the world around her.

As we both grew older, I began to feel that I played a minor but useful role in her life. As a neighbour rather than family, it was relatively easy for me to love and affirm her, even when she was angry or abrasive. Our relationship became, in a small way, a place of forgiveness – a place where she was always already accepted and reconciled. When we were together she could take the risk, little by little, of lowering her guard against the world, and relax, even practise a little trust and hope. I don't know how much difference our friendship made in the end – most of the time, we never do know – but my sense was that it made a little. I know that her company and her affection were both a delight and an education to me.

The way my relationship with Jane grew was a happy accident, possible because we were neighbours over many years. But it taught me a precious lesson about reconciliation. Sometimes what people need from us, and what we can offer them, is forgiveness, not for something they did to us, but for something others did to them or they did to others long ago and in another place.

The group agreed that forgiveness, and the change that goes with it, are usually time-consuming processes. They may take a lifetime. Often they are not finished – sometimes they are barely begun – before somebody dies. Forgiveness may take generations. Very often, no one person can offer all the forgiveness another person needs.

That's why it's helpful to live and act in communities: so that we can share the work of forgiveness and reconciliation, in any one lifetime and across lifetimes. But ultimately, nothing we can do for one another approaches the scope of what is possible for God. Final forgiveness, final reconciliation, final freedom from conflict and hurt and pain come not from any human community, but from God.

When we forgive each other – when we make for each other a place and time in which we are loved and affirmed and have space to be reconciled – then we are representing God in the world, in one of the strongest ways possible for a human being. We are showing someone visibly and tangibly that forgiveness is with them, and that reconciliation is always open to them.

It is a challenge to support this level of openness and love towards other people, especially if they have hurt us or we know that they have hurt others. We can only do it to the extent that we are relying not on ourselves and our own resources, spiritual, mental and emotional, but on God. To be forgiving people who work for reconciliation, we must be effective channels for the Holy Spirit. The Pentecost group's discussions, therefore, turned next to the question of what it means to be a channel for the Holy Spirit, and what aspects of our lives hamper us when we want to be one.

Questions for discussion

- Do you think that forgiveness should be given before, after or hand-in-hand with repentance?
- Can groups share the work of forgiveness with individuals?
- When do you find forgiveness hardest?

5

Freeing the Spirit

<hr>

If there was one thing the Pentecost discussion group agreed about from the first meeting, it was that the centre of all Christian life is our relationship with God. This is both an intuition in the hearts of believers, and the core of the teaching of Jesus in the Gospels. The Gospels show Jesus telling all kinds of people, from his closest followers to hostile opponents, to love God and love their neighbours. Wherever we stand, in imagination, in the scenes of the New Testament – among the disciples, or at the edge of a crowd, or alone with Jesus on a deserted road – we hear the same lesson. Every time we hear it, the commandment to love God comes first.

We saw our relationship with God as the foundation and power-house of our lives of ministry. We began by looking at some of the ways the New Testament shows us of strengthening it.

Attending to our relationship with God

The simplest way to strengthen our relationship with God is by offering God our trust and obedience directly, as we are taught and shown how to do throughout the Gospels. 'Let it be with me according to your word', says Mary to the angel (Luke 1.38). Jesus tells his followers, 'Do not worry about your life . . . strive first for the kingdom of God and his righteousness . . .' (Matt. 6.25, 33), and teaches his disciples to pray, 'your will be done' (Matt. 6.10). In the garden of Gethsemane, Jesus himself prays: 'Abba, Father, for you all things are possible; remove this cup from me; yet, not what I want, but what you want' (Mark. 14.36).

Another way is to try to follow Jesus' example. Jesus tells his disciples that following his example is the way to follow him. 'If any want to become my followers, let them deny themselves and take up their cross and follow me' (Mark 8.34). At the Last Supper, Jesus, blessing and sharing bread and wine, tells his disciples, 'Do this in remembrance of me' (1 Cor. 11.24–25).

Following Jesus' example is described traditionally as imitating Christ. It might mean trying to have something of the same radical trust in God and faithfulness to God that Jesus had; proclaiming the nearness of the kingdom of heaven as Jesus did; practising the same love and compassion as Jesus did; or speaking out against violations of God's love like injustice and hypocrisy as Jesus did. No one, of course, can be exactly like Christ. In *The Imitation of Christ*, Thomas à Kempis warns us not to let imitating Christ make us conceited:

> Whoever desires to understand and take delight in the words of Christ must strive to conform his whole life to Him . . . A true understanding and humble estimate of oneself is the highest and most valuable of all lessons . . . Should you see another person openly doing evil, or carrying out a wicked purpose, do not on that account consider yourself better than him, for you cannot tell how long you will remain in a state of grace. We are all frail; consider none more frail than yourself . . .   (Ch. 1, 2)

Some members of the group were uneasy about the idea of imitating Christ because it sounded like imagining that we *were* like Christ, or as if we could know what Jesus would have done in every situation which faces us in our own lives. For Thomas, the way we avoid that is by doing the most basic thing that Jesus did, and submitting ourselves to God. 'The more humble and obedient to God a man is, the more wise and at peace he will be in all that he does' (Ch. 4).

St Paul describes the way he follows Christ in slightly different language. He has died to his old life and now it is Christ who lives in him and works through him:

I have been crucified with Christ; and it is no longer I who live, but it is Christ who lives in me. And the life I now live in the flesh I live by faith in the Son of God, who loved me and gave himself for me.   (Gal. 2.19–20)

Elsewhere, Paul uses the opposite image to convey the same idea: he has put on Christ or is in Christ. 'So if anyone is in Christ, there is a new creation ... So we are ambassadors for Christ, since God is making his appeal through us' (2 Cor. 5.17, 20).

These images were picked up by the writers of some of the Acts of the Martyrs, to express the power we have to overcome evil and suffering when Christ is in us or we put on Christ. When Sanctus of Lyons, for example, was martyred in about AD 177, he was brutally tortured, but refused to renounce his faith. He was so brave, his biographer said, because Christ was in him. 'Christ suffering in him achieved great glory, overwhelming the devil, and showing as an example to all the others that nothing is to be feared where the Father's love is, nothing painful where we find Christ's glory.'[1] A slave girl called Blandina, martyred in the same persecution, is described as putting on Christ, in order to overcome the devil, inspire her fellow Christians and win the crown of immortality.[2]

Both these images tell us that once we accept Christ, our lives are no longer our own. We speak and act on Christ's behalf. As St Teresa of Avila expresses it:

Christ has no body but yours,
No hands, no feet on earth but yours,
Yours are the eyes with which he looks
Compassion on this world,
Yours are the feet with which he walks to do good,
Yours are the hands with which he blesses all the world.

This idea brings imitating Christ closer to another image of Christian life which runs through the New Testament and later tradition: that we hope to allow the Spirit of God to work through us in the world. It may be helpful to think of Christ in us, or ourselves in Christ, as another way of talking about the Holy

Spirit in us and acting through us. As aspects of God, Christ and the Spirit can't be separated, either from each other or from God the Creator.

All the Gospels tell us that Jesus himself received the Spirit of God at his baptism. According to St Luke (4.18–19), Jesus begins his ministry in the synagogue at Nazareth by reading from Isaiah, 'The Spirit of the Lord is upon me, because he has anointed me to bring good news to the poor . . .' In St John's Gospel, Jesus promises the disciples that he will not leave them without sending the Holy Spirit to teach, comfort and inspire them:

> 'If you love me, you will keep my commandments. And I will ask the Father, and he will give you another Advocate, to be with you for ever. This is the Spirit of truth . . . the Advocate, the Holy Spirit, whom the Father will send in my name, will teach you everything, and remind you of all that I have said to you.'   (John 14.15–17, 26)

The Acts of the Apostles begin with the disciples preparing for and receiving the Holy Spirit at the feast of Pentecost in Jerusalem (Acts 2.1–4).

Because Jesus receives the Spirit at his baptism, but his followers much later and not at baptism, there is some debate about whether Christians nowadays should hope to receive the Spirit at baptism, or whether it is a separate gift which may come to us at any time. But if we think of the Spirit as the power of God working through us, then perhaps, for most of us, the Spirit comes as love and faith and reconciliation come – bit by bit, throughout our lives, as we gradually learn to put more trust in God and give our lives more fully to God.

All these descriptions of our relationship with Christ and the Spirit have one thing in common: they have a very practical purpose. The Spirit comes upon Jesus and the apostles so that they can preach the good news and bring the kingdom of heaven closer. 'All this is from God,' St Paul writes, 'who reconciled us to himself through Christ, and has given us the ministry of reconciliation . . . So we are ambassadors for Christ, since God is making his appeal through us; we entreat you on behalf of Christ, be reconciled to God' (2 Cor. 5.18, 20). If we aspire to follow the example of the first apostles and become apostles for our own age, we need to do everything we can to enable Christ, and the Spirit, to work through us.

Unhelpful passions

There are many practical ways of attending every day to our relationship with God, some of which the discussion group would come back to in later weeks. First, though, we focused on the things which make it difficult to follow Christ.

We all felt that it can be hard for human beings, damaged and discouraged as we are by the harm others do to us, and self-estranged from God by the harm we do to others, to recognize and accept God's love and forgiveness. Even when we begin to do so, all that damage and potential for harm don't usually melt away. They tend to be waiting, just below the surface of our faith or round the first corner of our pilgrimage, to trip us up and discourage us. If we hope to follow Christ and become a channel for God's love in the world, then we need to recognize, to face and let go of the things which block the action of the Spirit in us.

Tradition offers several lists of things which block the action of the Spirit. They are widely known as 'sins', but that word has unhelpful overtones of the most negative strands in Christian tradition. Some early Christian writers talk about 'passions' rather than 'sins', or what we might call, specifically, negative or unhelpful passions.

Ideas and ways of speaking or acting which block the action of the Spirit are 'passions' because they are so often driven by emotion. Like any physical passion, they buffet us about with their emotional force. They make us suffer, and 'suffering' is the root meaning (in Latin) of the word 'passion'. They are unhelpful because they make it more difficult for us to love God and one another.

Perhaps the oldest Christian list of unhelpful passions is Paul's list of the 'works of the flesh' (which he contrasts with the 'fruits of the Spirit') in Galatians 5.19–21:

Now the works of the flesh are obvious: fornication, impur-
ity, licentiousness, idolatry, sorcery, enmities, strife, jealousy,
anger, quarrels, dissentions, factions, envy, drunkenness, carousing, and things like these. I am warning you, as I warned you
before: those who do such things will not inherit the kingdom
of God.

This is probably not intended to be an exhaustive list, but some
trends emerge from it. Paul seems to divide the works of the flesh
broadly into three kinds: offences against God, like idolatry and
sorcery; offences against other people, like enmity, strife, jealousy
and faction; and offences against our own bodies and minds, such
as drunkenness and carousing.

The most famous, later list of unhelpful passions is the list of
so-called 'seven deadly sins', which was codified by Pope Gregory
the Great (*c*.540–604), though similar lists were made earlier by,
among others, Evagrius the Hermit in the fourth century and St
John Cassian in the fifth. The seven deadly sins are pride, covetous-
ness, lust, envy, gluttony, anger and sloth, which is sometimes called
accidie or despair. Lust, envy and gluttony are all forms of greed,
so our discussion group thought we might put them together
and shorten the list to four. To these we added fear, which stops
us from taking risks with our selves and our lives for the sake of
the gospel. All these are passions because they rage in us, embroil
us in negative situations and cause us to damage ourselves, other
people and our relationship with God.

The first Christians and, later, founders of monastic orders,
were acutely aware that when groups of people live close together
and are all working hard at their spiritual lives, their weaknesses
and unhelpful passions quickly come bubbling to the surface. For
the sake of each person's spiritual development, and the survival
of the community as a whole, all communities need to address
people's unhelpful passions and try to defuse and dismantle them.
The same is true nowadays. If we want to act as a channel for the
action of Christ and the Spirit of God in the world, then we'll
need to identify and try to defuse the things that stop the Spirit

acting freely in us. Monastic writings are a rich source of advice about how to recognize and tackle unhelpful passions in oneself and other members of one's community.

In his *Institutes*, Cassian explores eight unhelpful passions: gluttony, fornication, avarice, anger, sadness, anxiety, vainglory and pride. Pride is above all the sin of believing that we do not need God (*Inst.* 12.4.1), and it has many symptoms:

> First, [the person] is loud in speech and bitter in silence; in joy his laughter is thoroughly immoderate; in seriousness he is irrationally sad; his response is grudging, his speech glib; his words erupt all over the place from his heart without any gravity. He is without patience, devoid of love, ready to inflict abuse but not to take it, slow to obedience except when it suits his will and desire, deaf to exhortation, weak in restraining his desires, adamantly unyielding to others, and constantly fighting for his own views without ever giving in to or accepting those of others. And so he becomes incapable of receiving good advice and in every situation relies entirely on his own judgement rather than that of his elders.
>
> (*Inst.* 12.29.2–3, my translation)

The cure is to remember constantly that we cannot do anything, above all anything good, without God's help. Like Christ, we should say, 'I am not able to do anything of myself, but my father who abides in me himself does the works' (*Inst.* 12.17.1).

Cassian's monks often tell him they would have no trouble at all avoiding the unhelpful passions, if only other people would not get in their way and annoy them. This, he says, misses the point. Other people have as much right to exist as we do ourselves. Not everyone naturally gets on with everyone else, but Jesus told us to love *all* our neighbours. The business of life, and of faith, is to get on with people, not to run away from them. Besides, avoiding annoying people isn't a cure for unhelpful passions. If we suffer from anger, for instance, we'll find something to get angry about, even when we're alone.

I remember when I was living in the desert, being so furious with my pen, when either its thickness or its thinness annoyed me, or with my knife, when it had a blunt edge and would not cut properly something that needed cutting, or with my flint, if it produced a spark of fire too slowly when I was in a hurry to read, that I couldn't ventilate and get rid of my turbulence of mind except by cursing inanimate objects or the devil. So for the perfection of our reason, it is not enough that there should be no other people around to get angry with, because if we have not learned patience, we can get equally angry even with dumb objects. And if there is anger in our heart, it will not let us possess a steady state of tranquillity, nor to be without residual vices.

(Inst. 8.19.2–3)

Freeing the Spirit

When people are damaged and imperfect beings – when we suffer from unhelpful passions – it is often because we have been hurt in childhood, at a moment of special vulnerability, or repeatedly over time, or because harm done to others has been passed down to us in the form of damaging behaviour or negative expectations. We need to face and tackle this damage in ourselves to prevent ourselves from passing it on to others, and to help God to work through us and pass on good things to others.

Many of the tools we use to attend to other people and forgive them, can also be used on ourselves. At the same time, everything we learn when trying to identify and defuse our own unhelpful passions, helps us when we try to understand and help others.

We can identify five steps in the process of tackling unhelpful passions.

Step 1: Attentiveness

We have seen how important it is to be attentive to other people. But it is just as important to be attentive to ourselves, and notice which unhelpful passions we are suffering from at any one moment. We can assume that we will suffer from them all at some point!

The power of the traditional lists of sins to grip our imagination comes from the fact that the things they describe are endemic in everyday life. Casting my mind back over the last few weeks as I type, I see I've been annoyed about at least six different things, small and large. A close friend had a serious operation, and I worried about the results. And I definitely desired a jacket I saw in a shop last week. Continuing down the list – yes, I've suffered from all the passions recently. Which, alas, is just what I'd expect. If we think there's a passion we don't suffer from, then we are almost certainly fooling ourselves.

When we attend to our unhelpful passions, we are practising love towards ourselves. Jesus told us to 'love your neighbour as yourself' (Luke 10.27). Just as other people are more likely to be able to let go of their unhelpful passions, to seek and accept forgiveness and reconciliation, if we show that we love them and believe in them, so we're more likely to be able to let go of our own unhelpful passions if we love and affirm ourselves. Hating and punishing ourselves for not being perfect only makes us feel worse, and that may lead us to think either that we are not worth saving, or to despair and say, to hell with the world! Either way, our unhelpful passions will flourish and we'll become unhappier and more destructive, not happier and more loving people.

Step 2: Understanding our passions

The second step, once we're aware of our passions, is to understand why we are feeling them.

I have a neighbour who often parks his truck outside my house. In the mornings, he likes to warm it up by letting the engine run for several minutes while he cleans the windscreen or sorts out his tools for the day. The exhaust fills my study with smelly fumes and annoys me a good deal.

But when I look more closely at my irritation, it's not obvious why I am so annoyed. I don't like the smell and the fumes, of course. But I know that when he drives off, they will dissipate very quickly. I don't suppose they're seriously damaging my health.

As I think about it, I begin to see that part of what annoys me is that he is being thoughtless – towards me and towards the environment. Oxford is polluted enough, I grumble to myself, without people running their engines while they're parked. So why haven't I asked him to stop? Digging deeper, I find several reasons. I'm worried that I'm overreacting, and my irritation is my own fault. I'm afraid that if I tackle him, he'll ignore me, and then I'll feel worse – intentionally as well as unintentionally treated with disrespect. It occurs to me that perhaps he *has* to run his engine for some reason I don't understand, and I'm embarrassed to show my ignorance by asking. And I'm so annoyed that I'm afraid I'll overstate my complaint, and since he is in other ways a good neighbour, I don't want to upset him.

You may feel that all this could be very simply solved by my going out and explaining politely to my neighbour that he is filling my house with fumes, and would it be possible for him to stop? Now I have analysed my anger, I think so too.

And that's the point. Most of us, most of the time, don't understand our passions. As a result, we get trapped in them and can't see a way out. When we do take time to examine how we feel, we often find that even passions with apparently simple causes are quite complicated, because they feed not just on our present situation, but on problems and passions we have suffered in the past. Then we need to separate out our present problem from past problems, and deal with them one at a time.

Step 3: Separating out the causes of passions

I have established that I don't like exhaust fumes, but that several other passions have got entangled with my reaction to my neighbour. I am afraid that I'm not worth protecting from exhaust fumes. I am afraid of being treated with disrespect and not being able to do anything about it. I am afraid of showing ignorance. And I'm afraid of my own temper, and don't want to hurt people with it.

Having disentangled all these emotions, I can see that my neighbour's behaviour is a small problem, which should be easily fixed. The bigger problem is the deeper-rooted passions which got dragged into the situation. I suspect that they are all problems I've had for a long time – quite likely since childhood.

My next task is to reflect on those. When, for instance, did I learn that low sense of entitlement? When was I treated with disrespect and couldn't do anything about it? When did I learn that it's bad to show ignorance?

Memory immediately produces an instance of disrespect that still rankles after more than 30 years. I was seven years old, and my class at school was drawing pictures of our homes and gardens. I put in some green euphorbias, which grew in our front garden. The teacher called me up to her desk. 'Why have you drawn green flowers? There are no green flowers!' 'Th-there are – green flowers', I stumbled. 'What green flowers are there?' the teacher demanded. I was dumb. I didn't know their name. She made me go back and colour them red. What I remember most is the triumph in her eyes. She, an adult, was delighted to have scored off a seven-year-old. I was shocked to the core and I never forgave her.

It was the first, but sadly not the last time I saw a teacher take pleasure in putting a pupil down. We wouldn't have dared to complain at the time. But now, as an adult, I always overreact when I think I'm being treated disrespectfully. It is surely time to deal with this particular fragment of suffering.

Step 4: Letting go

The fourth step, once we have worked out what unhelpful passions are hurting us and where they come from, is to practise letting them go.

Mulling over the incident of the green flowers, I remember that my teacher was elderly. She must have been close to retirement. She was probably tired, and maybe had run out of patience with children. Perhaps, in the past, she had suffered at the hands of clever people – had been shown up or put down – and perhaps her behaviour to her pupils was a way of trying to compensate for her own suffering. She certainly wasn't unkind or unfair all the time. As far as I remember, she was a good teacher. And she must have died many years ago, and is at rest. I'm sure she wouldn't want her suffering or her unkindness to go on damaging the world through me. I don't want it to, either. I will let her go in peace, and hope to find my own peace as I do.

Making that decision is an important step, but it's rarely the end of the story. My teacher's action made a mark on me which doesn't disappear the moment I begin to understand it. Over the years, overreacting to perceived disrespect has become a habit. I shall have to watch myself, and the next time it happens, I will remind myself that I have found and faced the root of that particular passion, and that I need not suffer from it any more. The next time it happens, I shall do the same. And the next. And the time after that – until gradually, a new habit takes the place of the old and my anger towards my teacher withers away.

This, of course, is a very simple example. The hurt was a small one, and it is relatively easy for me to believe that my teacher didn't mean to hurt me, but was reacting to some previous suffering of her own. Many of our passions have much larger, more complicated and more painful causes, and sometimes the people who hurt us really intended to hurt. Then the work we have to do is much bigger and more difficult and may take much longer. In some cases, we may need professional help. We may also need to talk our feelings and experiences through informally with a good listener.

Step 5: Becoming a firebreak

Letting go of some deep-rooted passions may be a lifetime's work. But while we are doing it, we can take Step 5 at the same time. We can make a decision that, however damaged and imperfect we are, we will do everything we can not to pass on that damage to other people. And we won't wait till we become perfect: we'll start doing it now.

This is what was described at the beginning of the last chapter as acting like a firebreak to evil, and it is one of the most life-transforming ways in which we can follow Christ. When we take this step, we are putting our trust in God in a profound and radical way. We are saying, 'I am not fully healed. I still struggle to forgive and be forgiven. I don't know whether my unhelpful passions will ever leave me completely. But I believe that the love and power of God for reconciliation are infinite. I believe that God can and does work in and through imperfect human beings. I put my trust in that healing power, and I put myself in God's hands. Lord, help me to become part of the healing process.'

Deciding not to pass on our suffering, but to become part of the healing process is, paradoxically, often one of the biggest steps we take towards our own healing. Perhaps it's because seeing ourselves offering love and reconciliation to others boosts our confidence that love and reconciliation really do change people's lives. Nothing strengthens our faith in Christ, whom we can't see, more than seeing the traces of Christ's work among us – in other people and in ourselves. Allowing God to work through us helps us to allow God to work in us.

More tools for defusing unhelpful passions

If we let them, our passions feed on us and grow at our expense. In extreme cases, they can take over large parts of our lives, soaking up time and energy, threatening our health, relationships or livelihood. Being a slave to any unhelpful passion is exhausting, depressing and destructive. As soon as we begin to let them go, our hearts grow lighter, we have more energy, we feel happier in ourselves, we find it easier to like other people, and the world becomes a brighter and more hopeful place.

Above all, unhelpful passions get in the way of our relationships with God, and each other, by distracting and confusing us, and shifting our focus away from love and reconciliation onto things that alienate us from one another. The more we let them go, the more energy and clarity of mind and heart we have to act as Christ's hands and feet in the world.

The Vietnamese Zen Buddhist monk and teacher Thich Nhat Hanh has written about how to defuse anger, in terms which apply equally well to all unhelpful passions. *Anger: Buddhist Wisdom for Cooling the Flames* is as relevant to Christians as Buddhists, and the exercises which Thich Nhat Hanh recommends are similar to forms of Christian meditation. Here, he discusses how we begin to address angry feelings:

> When someone says or does something that makes us angry, we suffer . . .
>
> Anger is like a howling baby, suffering and crying. The baby needs his mother to embrace him. You are the mother for your baby, your anger . . .
>
> Embrace your anger with a lot of tenderness. Your anger is not your enemy; your anger is your baby. It's like your stomach or your lungs. Every time you have some trouble in your lungs or stomach, you don't think of throwing them away. The same is true of your anger. You accept your anger because you know you can take care of it; you can transform it into positive energy . . .
>
> The organic gardener doesn't think of throwing away the garbage. She knows that she needs the garbage. She is capable of transforming the garbage into compost, so that the compost can turn into lettuce, cucumbers, radishes, and flowers again . . . You are a kind of gardener, an organic gardener . . .
>
> If you see elements of garbage in you, like fear, despair, and hatred, don't panic. As a good organic gardener . . . you can face this: 'I recognize that there is garbage in me. I am going to transform this garbage into nourishing compost that can make love reappear.'
>
> . . . [P]ractice has two phases. The first phase is embracing and recognizing, 'My dear anger, I know you are there, I am taking good care of you.' The second phase is to look deeply into the nature of your anger to see how it has come about.
>
> (pp. 23, 27–8, 30–32)[3]

Thich Nhat Hanh invites us to examine the causes of our destructive passions, and to recognize how our own and other people's suffering in the past has established negative habits of thought and behaviour in us. We can then work to separate the past from the present and future, to resolve our past suffering and to let our destructive passions go.

Anthony de Mello, a Jesuit priest and well-known spiritual director who lived and worked in India for many years, wrote a number of books about contemplative prayer and about how, using contemplative techniques, we can learn to let go of our unhelpful passions and heal ourselves. His approach is very similar to that of Thich Nhat Hanh, though it is influenced by Hinduism rather than Buddhism, and also owes something to Western psychology. Here, in *Sadhana: A Way to God*, he suggests a way of tackling all kinds of unhelpful passions:

> People sometimes carry with them wounds from the past that still rankle. With the passage of time the rankling may no longer be felt, but the harmful effect of the wound will still persist.
>
> It is helpful to return to the events that produced ... negative feelings so as to drain them of any harmful effect they have on you today. Return to some scene in the past where you felt pain or grief or hurt or fear or bitterness ... Relive the event ... But this time seek and find the presence of the Lord in it ... in what way is he present there? Or, imagine that the Lord himself is taking part in the event ... What role is he playing? ... Speak to him. Ask him the meaning of what is happening ... Listen to what he says in reply ...
>
> An unwillingness to forgive others for the real or imaginary wrongs they have done us is a poison that affects our health – physical, emotional and spiritual ... It generally helps, first of all, to get the resentment out of your system. For this, imagine you see the person you resent there in front of you. Tell him/her of your resentment, express your anger as force-fully as you can ... After expressing all your resentment, and only after, look at the whole incident that caused the resent-ment from the other person's point of view. Take his place:

how does the incident look when seen through his/her eyes? Realize too that people do not [usually] hurt you as a result of malice. Even supposing an intention to hurt, this was a result of a misperception of reality, or of some deep-rooted unhappiness in the other person. Genuinely happy people are not unkind. Moreover, it is quite likely that you person-ally are not the target of other people's attacks.

(pp. 80–1, 83–4)[4]

When addressing unhelpful passions it is better to start with our own than with other people's. We all need a certain humility in dealing with each other's failings. No human being, in the sight of God, has the moral high ground. We are all imperfect, and need to remember it before we criticize other people for being imperfect.

All communities need ways in which people can bring their problems and criticisms of each other out into the open. But we always need to distinguish between times when other people are saying or doing something really destructive, times when they are just being themselves in a way which happens to irritate us because we are temperamentally different, and times when their behaviour is reasonable in itself, but for some reason reminds us of something else, said or done by somebody else, which makes us angry or upset. Attacking someone who just happens to irritate us, or who says or does something which reminds us of someone completely different, only makes both ourselves and him or her feel worse.

Most of us don't find it easy to identify, investigate and tackle our unhelpful passions on our own. It's hard work to face one's failings, to trace them to their source and begin to defuse them. We need affirmation and encouragement on the way.

One of the main things the Pentecost discussion group did was one of the main things that any religious community does: to support its members as they make their individual journeys of faith. Knowing that other people are on the same journey as ourselves, doing the same work, is always encouraging, and we can help one another by listening, sharing our experiences and forgiving each other when, despite our best efforts, our unresolved passions get the better of us.

Communities also develop together – through worship, prayer and discussion groups, practical initiatives to help their neighbours, and much more. Some people may find it helpful to have a 'spiritual director' – a particular person to talk to about how their religious life is developing, who may also give advice out of their own experience. If spiritual direction feels too formal or one can't find someone suitable, there may be one or two people who can simply be friends and conversation-partners on the spiritual journey. The 'Further resources' section at the end of this book gives some suggestions for finding different types of religious communities, spiritual directors and other resources.

Questions for discussion

- Do you find the term 'passions' more or less helpful than 'sins'? Why?
- Discuss the passage from Thich Nhat Hanh. Do you find it a helpful addition to Christian thinking on unhelpful passions?
- How does our relationship with Christ and the Holy Spirit help us to tackle unhelpful passions?

6

Living prayer

———•◦•———

Ways of attending

When we attend to our relationship with God by tackling unhelpful passions, we are practising one kind of prayer. To pray means simply to pay attention to God. 'Raising our heart to God' is how one writer describes it.[1] We may be expressing our love for God, repenting of things we have done wrong or asking for help. We may be blessing someone or giving thanks. We may be practising obeying God, imitating Christ or letting ourselves become a channel for the Holy Spirit. We may be experiencing the presence of God or waiting hopefully to experience it. They are all forms of prayer.

The members of the Pentecost group came with very different experiences of prayer. Some people didn't pray much, if ever, outside church. Some prayed when they felt they needed to. A few prayed every day. Several people said they found the idea of praying rather intimidating or a bit of a mystery. They were never sure if they were doing the right thing or doing it the right way. So we began by discussing what prayer is, and then some of the group described what they do when they pray.

Some people pray by reading a chapter of the Bible each day, slowly and meditatively, letting the words speak to them, and perhaps say things they have never heard in them before. This is sometimes known as *lectio divina*, 'spiritual reading'.

Some people say the offices of morning and evening prayer, and sometimes midday prayer and compline last thing at night, or even all seven traditional offices of the monastic day. Anglicans can choose between morning and evening prayer from the Book of Common Prayer, the same offices in a modern prayer book such as *Common Worship*, liturgies developed by (often ecumenical) communities such as the Taizé Community or the Iona Community, and the offices of several monastic orders.

Some people use more or less fixed forms of prayer, which might include the Lord's Prayer and intercessions, versions of which appear in all prayer books. There are many collections of prayers in print – prayers from around the world, from every period of history, and from different denominations. Everyone uses 'arrow prayers' from time to time too – the short, snappy, informal prayers we send up in moments of acute need. 'Lord, help me!' 'Give me patience!'

However we pray, we need to find a balance between routine and freedom. As with most activities, from cooking to painting watercolours to playing a sport, we get better at it by practising regularly. But occasionally we need to break out of that discipline and let ourselves do whatever we like. When I was a music student, I started practice every day with two hours of scales and exercises, which was the best way to improve my technique. Occasionally, though, I would rebel and, after a quick warm-up, go straight to a piece of music. Now it's the same with prayer. I have a routine which I practise every day – but occasionally I give myself a day off or do something completely different.

The most important thing about prayer is that it should become part of everyday life and be mixed in with all our other activities. When we're immersed in caring for a family, looking for work, pursuing a career, developing our talents, or all of them at once, that's when we most need to stay in touch with God. And we can use prayer as a yardstick against which to measure our other activities. Whatever we're doing, we can ask ourselves, 'Can I do this prayerfully, as an expression of God's love for the world and my love for God?' If the answer is yes, all's well. If the answer is no, we might want to think about why we're doing it.

Our Pentecost group was especially interested in exploring kinds of prayer which we could take with us as we went about our everyday lives. We focused on two: contemplative prayer and prayer without ceasing.

Contemplative prayer

Contemplative prayer is also known as meditation, and it is practised in many religious traditions (and in secular contexts too). It is a way of expressing our devotion to God and our desire always to be as close to God as possible.

In this classic, anonymous English text from the fourteenth century, a mystic describes the impulse that called him or her to contemplative prayer, and calls us to it too:

Lift up your heart to God with humble love: and mean God himself, and not what you can get out of him. Indeed, hate to think of anything but God himself, so that nothing occupies your mind or will, but only God. Try to forget all created things that he ever made, and the purpose behind them, so that your thought and longing do not turn or reach out to them in general or in particular. Let them go, and pay no attention to them. It is the work of the soul that pleases God most . . .

But now you will ask me, 'How am I to think of God himself, and what is he?' and I cannot answer you except to say, 'I do not know!' For with this question you have brought me into the same darkness, the same cloud of unknowing where I want you to be! For though we through the grace of God can know fully about all other matters, and think about them – yes, even the very works of God himself – yet of God himself can no man think. Therefore I will leave on one side everything I can think; and choose for my love that thing which I cannot think! Why? Because he may well be loved, but not thought. By love he can be caught and held, but by thinking, never . . .

So if you are to stand and not to fall, never give up your firm intention: beat away at this cloud of unknowing between you and God with that sharp dart of longing love. Hate to think about anything less than God, and let nothing whatever distract you from this purpose.

(The Cloud of Unknowing, 3, 6, 12)

Focusing our attention, our mind and heart exclusively and steadily on any one thing doesn't come naturally to most of us. It takes practice. Happily, there are now many teachers, courses and books available to help us begin, some of which are listed in 'Further resources'.

It is probably easiest to start by sitting on a hard chair or cross-legged on the floor. It helps to be physically comfortable but upright, with one hand cupped loosely in the other in one's lap.

We begin by focusing our mind on one thing. It can be a word, a picture, a sense of the presence of Christ, or any object chosen at random. (I was taught to meditate by focusing on a bobble in the carpet.) Some people follow their breaths, counting them repeatedly from one to ten. Others listen to the sounds around them, and then tune in to the silence between the sounds.

At first, most people find their thoughts wandering off every second or two. As soon as that happens, we let the intruding thoughts go, gently, and bring our mind back to its focal point. Gradually, we learn to concentrate for longer. At first, practice sessions of 20 minutes or so are enough for most people; day by day, they can be extended to half an hour, an hour, or more.

For some meditators, the heart of contemplative prayer consists in experiencing the presence of Christ. For others, it is about waiting to sense the presence or power of God. Some people focus on bringing their heart into harmony with the harmony of God and God's creation.

Stilling the mind is the first step in contemplative prayer, but once we have become, if not completely still, at least stiller than usual, we can also use the focus it gives us to help us think more deeply about a person, an image, an idea or a text. At this point, contemplation meets other forms of prayer and *lectio divina*. We explore whatever we are thinking about slowly, taking our time and looking at it from all angles. One point of focus can last for several sessions, or one session can have more than one point of focus.

As we get better at stilling and focusing our minds, other things begin to happen. Our breaths get longer and slower. Heart rate and blood pressure drop. Some people stop being aware of their body at all, or become acutely aware of it – every inch of skin and every pulse of blood. The body may start to feel heavy, like a lump of clay, or very light, like a balloon, or like a fountain of water. We may feel as if we're floating above it. Consciousness may narrow to a single point, and pour itself away into nothingness. Some people feel they are flying, or see hallucinations – bright colours, patterns or images. Others feel a profound peace and happiness. All these phenomena are normal when the mind is freed from its everyday whirlwind of thoughts and emotions. They are interesting and often enjoyable, but they are not important, and it doesn't matter whether they come or go. What matters is always and only God.

Most of us need to begin practising contemplative prayer by sitting down to do it and nothing else. But once we have some experience in stilling our minds and focusing on God, contemplation becomes portable. We can learn to summon that calm concentration in the middle of a busy day, between or even during other activities.

Contemplation in action

Over the past few years, contemplative prayer has become the centre of my religious practice. I try to spend some time each day sitting and stilling my mind. I read a chapter of the Bible slowly and reflectively. But what has made the most difference to my everyday life has been taking contemplation to work.

Like so many jobs these days, mine is infested with busyness. We all always seem to be dashing about, fitting too much in, combating tiredness with coffee and adrenaline. There's always a new batch of emails to answer, another meeting to attend, a new document to write, an unexpected crisis to deal with – beside our main work of teaching and doing research. (And if this is what life is like for university lecturers, I sometimes think, what is it like for transplant surgeons or politicians or CEOs of multi-national corporations?)

I try to defuse my busyness by looking for the stillness at the heart of the whirlwind of work, and the harmony within that stillness. In the morning, when I enter my office and put down my bag, I stop for a moment to tune in to the silence of the room. On the way to and from meetings, I look at the stones of the surrounding buildings, and imagine the subatomic oscillations humming among them, the universal music of their silence. I wait to hear those moments in a meeting when everyone pauses for breath between agenda items; the sense of a cadence after one student has left the room, before the next comes in. There is silence and stillness everywhere, if we listen for it – and within the stillness, hints of a deeper music.

The stillness outside finds and echoes the stillness inside us. Contemplation creates a kind of interior desert: a space inside ourselves which is a retreat from the world. We can carry that space everywhere we go. Whenever we need to, we can return to it for a moment or two, turning our hearts and minds from whatever we are doing, towards God.

Busyness is not the only challenge to contemplation. Having nothing to do can be just as difficult to handle as having too much to do – or it can be an equally rich source of prayerful stillness. Standing in supermarket queues, sitting in doctors' waiting rooms and waiting in airport lounges, have become some of the most prayerful spaces I know over the years.

At the same time, because contemplation is a tool for looking deeply into people and things, we can also use it to focus on our work and other activities. In earlier chapters, we have seen the importance of attentiveness, to ourselves, to other people and to God. Contemplative concentration helps us to be attentive to all our activities and the people we share them with, and to find the presence of God in them.

This is the state of mind which George Herbert celebrated and asked God for in his famous poem, 'The Elixir':

> Teach me, my God and King,
> In all things thee to see,
> And what I do in anything,
> To do it as for thee.
>
> A man that looks on glass,
> On it may stay his eye;
> Or if he pleaseth, through it pass,
> And then the heav'n espy.
>
> All may of thee partake:
> Nothing can be so mean,
> Which with his tincture (for thy sake)
> Will not grow bright and clean.
>
> A servant with this clause
> Makes drudgery divine:
> Who sweeps a room, as for thy laws,
> Makes that and th' action fine.

Herbert calls the ability to see God in everything, to be focused on God with part of ourselves in every moment of everyday life, the true philosopher's stone: 'the famous stone that turneth all to gold'. Using a different metaphor, we might call it a touchstone: something we touch, in imagination if not physically, throughout each day to remind us of the real centre and focus of our life.

A few people are called to full-time contemplation, but most of us are not. Even those who are usually spend only part of their lives in contemplation, or allow it to be interrupted by people who want to talk or learn from them. The stories of the desert fathers and mothers are full of occasions when some fellow monk or would-be follower tracks a contemplative to his or her desert retreat, wanting to talk. Sometimes the monk or nun runs away, but more often he or she allows his or her solitude to be interrupted.

> A brother came to a certain solitary: and when he was leaving
> him, he said, 'Forgive me, Father, for I have made you break
> your rule.' He replied, 'My rule is to receive you with hospi-
> tality and send you away in peace.'[2]

On the other hand, everyone, whatever kind of life they live, can
be a contemplative. Henri le Saux (1910–73), who took the Indian
name Abhishiktananda, was a Benedictine monk. He was inspired
by an encounter with Hindu traditions of contemplation to recover
related Christian traditions, which had fallen into disuse in the
West, especially among lay people. His short book, *Prayer*, is one
of the most influential writings in modern Western Christianity
on contemplative prayer, and how practising it transforms our
lives. In this passage, Abhishiktananda emphasizes not only that
everyone can be a contemplative, but that everyone, however they
live, can and should *also* be a full-time contemplative.

> Prayer is not a part-time occupation for any of Christ's
> disciples – nor indeed is it so for any truly religious man.
> There are not two classes of Christians, some whose whole
> life should be devoted to prayer – whom we might call 'full-
> time contemplatives' – and others whose life is to be engaged
> in various activities, in family or society, or even in studying
> and preaching the word of God, and who therefore can only
> be 'part-time' contemplatives.
>
> Indeed there are no 'part-time contemplatives', any more
> than there are part-time Christians or part-time men. From
> the day when we begin to believe in Christ and to acknow-
> ledge him as our Lord, there is not a single moment of our
> time – waking, sleeping, walking, sitting, working, teaching,
> eating, playing – which is not marked by the claim of God
> upon us and which has not to be lived in the name of Jesus,
> under the inspiration of the Holy Spirit, to the glory of the
> Father.
>
> To live in constant prayer, to lead a contemplative life, is
> nothing else than to live in the actual presence of God. Every
> man indeed, by the very fact that he exists, is already in the

presence of God. This is especially true of the Christian man, who has been called to know the ultimate secrets of divine life, since by his baptism he has become a sharer in the divine sonship of Jesus, his Master.[3]

George Herbert was an Anglican, Abhishiktananda a Roman Catholic. The understanding which they share of the intimate relationship between prayer and practical activity in everyday life crosses all denominations. The founder of Methodism, John Wesley (1703–91), writes in a similar vein in his *Plain Account of Christian Perfection*. Just before this passage, Wesley says that being 'perfect' does not mean that one is free from ignorance, mistake, temptation or 'a thousand infirmities necessarily connected with flesh and blood'. It does, though, mean that one should live every day prayerfully.

> This it is to be a perfect man, to be 'sanctified throughout'; even 'to have a heart so all-flaming with the love of God (to use Archbishop Usher's word), 'as continually to offer up every thought, word, and work, as a spiritual sacrifice, acceptable to God, through Christ'; in every thought of our hearts, in every word of our tongues, in every work of our hands, to 'show forth his praise, who hath called us out of darkness into his marvellous light.' Oh that both we, and all who seek the Lord Jesus in sincerity, may thus be made perfect in one! (Ch. 15)

Prayer without ceasing

Some of the Pentecost group liked the idea of spending time in silent contemplation. Others thought it would be tough. Most of us these days are not used to long periods of silence; there is so little of it in the world around us. Out of doors, there aren't many places where we can't hear the hum of traffic. Indoors, there is the noise of televisions and computers, kettles and washing machines and central heating . . . everywhere there are people and mobile phones and our own busy thoughts and activities. We are equally unused to focusing on one thing at a time. Multi-tasking has become a virtue: we expect to check our mail during meetings, text while walking down the street, eat while watching television, and play music while doing anything.

To practise sitting in silence, some of the group felt, was a big step, possibly too big to take all at once. It might be easier to start by focusing on something positive, such as an object, a word or phrase – something we could touch or say, and return to in the course of a day. So we began to talk about prayer without ceasing.

Traditionally, prayer without ceasing is a different discipline from contemplative prayer, but the two are closely related. Both help us to attend to God all the time. We can see in the quotations above that people who are deeply immersed in contemplative prayer also see it as a form of prayer without ceasing.

We usually start to pray without ceasing by choosing, or being given, a word, a phrase from the Bible, a prayer, or even a phrase of music, which nowadays is often called a mantra. The word 'mantra' is borrowed from Indian tradition, and like contemplative prayer, prayer without ceasing has close relatives in Indian religions, especially Buddhism and Hinduism. The point of a mantra is that it is short and memorable enough to be said over and over again, dozens, then hundreds, then thousands of times every day. Eventually, if we keep saying it, then the mantra sinks into us until it seems to be saying itself with every beat of our heart, every movement of our limbs and every thought that passes through our mind.

The mantra which is most closely associated with prayer without ceasing is the ancient 'Jesus prayer': 'Lord Jesus Christ, Son of God and Saviour, have mercy on me, a sinner.' Many people in recent years have learned using the one-word mantra *Maranatha*, which is mentioned by St Paul (1 Cor. 16.22) and derives from the Aramaic for, 'Come, Lord' or, 'Our Lord has come'.

The practice of prayer without ceasing is described in detail in the anonymous nineteenth-century Russian story, *The Way of a Pilgrim*. This classic of Russian Orthodox spirituality describes how in church one day, a man hears part of St Paul's first epistle to the Thessalonians (5.17), in which he tells the Thessalonians to 'pray without ceasing'. The man is inspired to try to find out what this means, and embarks on a pilgrimage from church to church, seeking enlightenment. After some time, he reaches a monastery, where a *starets*, a wise elder, teaches him the Jesus Prayer: 'Lord Jesus Christ, have mercy on me.' Here, the *starets* explains how to begin using the prayer:

> The *starets* opened the *Philokalia* [the collection of Orthodox spiritual texts of the fourth to the fifteenth centuries], selected a passage from Saint Simeon the New Theologian, and began to read, 'Find a quiet place to sit alone and in silence; bow your head and shut your eyes. Breathe softly, look with your mind into your heart; recollect your mind – that is, all your thoughts – and bring them down from your mind into your heart. As you breathe, repeat, "Lord Jesus Christ, have mercy on me" – either quietly with your lips, or only in your mind. Strive to banish all thoughts; be calm and patient, and repeat this exercise frequently.' . . .

The pilgrim finds himself a job guarding a kitchen garden, and settles down to practise praying. After a good start, however, he finds 'great inner heaviness, laziness, boredom and drowsiness' coming over him. He consults the *starets*, who explains that this is the 'kingdom of darkness' attacking him. He advises the pilgrim to persevere, and say the prayer at least three thousand times a day. The pilgrim follows his advice, and from three thousand times a day, increases his repetitions to six, then twelve thousand a day.

> I spent the entire summer continuously repeating the Jesus Prayer with my lips. I was very much at peace and often even dreamed that I was uttering this prayer . . .
>
> Finally, after a short time, I felt that the prayer began to move of its own accord from my lips into my heart. That is to say, it seemed as if my heart, while beating naturally, somehow began to repeat within itself the worlds of the prayer in rhythm with its natural beating: (1) Lord . . . (2) Jesus . . . (3) Christ . . . and so on. I stopped reciting the words of the

prayer with my lips and began to listen attentively to the words of my heart, remembering what my *starets* said about how pleasant this would be. Then I began to experience a delicate soreness in my heart, and my thoughts were filled with such a love for Jesus Christ that it seemed to me that if I were to see Him, I would throw myself down, embrace His feet, and never let them go, kissing them tenderly and tearfully. And I would thank Him for His love and mercy in granting such consolation through His name to His unworthy and sinful creature!

For a time, the pilgrim retreats into solitude, viewing the rest of the world benignly but not wanting to have much to do with it. Eventually, though, he begins to travel again, wandering through Russia. He has many adventures, physical and spiritual, meets all sorts of people and hears their stories, and becomes a spiritual teacher in his own right.[4]

Mantras can be woven into our daily lives in all sorts of ways. I have met people who have engraved their mantra on a piece of jewellery; tied it to the wheels of their bicycle; set it to a hummable tune; carried it on a piece of paper in their pocket; linked it with something tangible like a stone, which they can hold to help them focus. Nor are mantras and contemplative prayer the only ways of praying without ceasing. The Catholic practice of saying the rosary is closely related, and helpfully combines verbal prayers with something one can hold to help one focus.

To pray without ceasing, whether with a mantra or simply by holding oneself continually in the presence of God, has been one of the ideals of Christian life since St Paul gave the Thessalonians the advice which sent the Russian pilgrim on his lifelong journey: 'Rejoice always, pray without ceasing, give thanks in all circumstances; for this is the will of God in Christ Jesus for you' (1 Thess. 5.16–18). It is something we can all aspire to and all practise, taking time out of the day to remember our mantra – to step into the desert – to look through the glass of everyday life into heaven – to wait upon God and sense God's presence with us.

Over time, contemplation and prayer without ceasing have a powerful effect on everyday life. They allow us to step outside its busyness – its pressures, demands and provocations. They give us a time and place of calm, in which everything that is not essential falls away. Returning periodically to our contemplative space, we gradually disentangle ourselves from our established patterns of thought, feeling and action. It becomes easier to distinguish unhelpful passions, and to let them go. We see ourselves and each other more clearly, our hearts and minds less clouded by our habitual reactions to one another.

Our inner desert gives us occasional glimpses of the God's-eye view: heaven's perspective on our world. Under its uninterrupted light, material things become just temporary associations of particles and energies: endlessly changing and never changing; endlessly forming, dissolving and reforming as one another. Everything is itself and everything else. Nothing is permanent. Nothing is lost. Sound is just the buffer between silences, and silence is only a subtler kind of music. Everything is one, and what is one is in harmony, and harmony is love. Nothing matters but love. We find ourselves not only ready to be reconciled, to forgive one another and ask to be forgiven, but already reconciled; already one.

Dissolving our unhelpful passions and keeping ourselves unceasingly in the presence of God by contemplative prayer, are two sides of the process by which we try to be Christ-like, to be a free-flowing channel for the Holy Spirit.

Solitude and community

Solitude is emerging as a theme in several of the chapters of this book. Prophecy, forgiveness, the dissolving of unhelpful passions – all these aspects of Christian life and ministry tend to evolve after people have withdrawn from their ordinary lives and activities for periods of reflection. In general, to develop spiritually we need sometimes to step outside the everyday world. We need to spend time on our own, praying and looking deeply into the divine and the mundane.

Religious traditions, though, tend to be influenced by the culture they belong to, and both modern Western culture and modern Western Christianity put more emphasis on community than solitude. Social skills are highly regarded, and it is seen as a sign of success, in religious no less than in secular life, to be in demand. Being solitary or wanting to be alone are regarded as at best eccentric, and at worst a sign of abnormality. Even religious orders tend to view solitude as something which can only safely be tried after one has been part of a strong community for many years.

As a result, many people are uncomfortable with the idea that solitude and solitary communion with God are fundamental to our religious practice. They prefer to emphasize that we develop as Christians, as we develop as members of any society, in community, by learning from each other and from the wisdom of tradition. They mistrust the idea that a single person, in solitary prayer, might encounter God or come to understand their faith more deeply than they could in other contexts.

This feeling is understandable, but it overlooks the strong theme of solitude running through Christian tradition, in which individuals come into closer communion with God, and are inspired, by retiring into solitude – often physically into the desert – to pray, wait and listen for God. It is part of our inheritance from Judaism, and has been richly added to over the centuries. It is there in stories of the prophets who withdraw from society at the call of God, in the life of Jesus who often goes into the desert or up a mountain to pray, and in the practice of early nuns and monks who retreat, often alone, to spend more of their lives in prayer.

It is from desert places and times, whether external or internal, literal or symbolic, that many of the most powerful revelations and teachings of our tradition have emerged. In recent centuries, St John of the Cross and George Fox are just two of those who have identified their inspiration as coming from times when they were literally or metaphorically alone in the wilderness. Here, from his Journal for 1646 and 1647, are parts of George Fox's description of the wilderness years before he found his vocation:

Now during the time that I was at Barnet a strong temptation to despair came over me. And then I saw how Christ was tempted, and mighty troubles I was in. And sometimes I kept myself retired to my chamber, and often walked solitary in the Chase there, to wait upon the Lord . . . I was about twenty years of age when these exercises came upon me, and some years I continued in that condition, in great trouble; and fain I would have put it from me. And I went to many a priest to look for comfort but found no comfort from them . . .

About the beginning of the year 1647, I was moved of the Lord to go into Derbyshire, where I met with some friendly people, and had many discourses with them . . . But my troubles continued, and I was often under great temptations; and I fasted much, and walked abroad in solitary places many days, and often took my Bible and went and sat in hollow trees and lonesome places till night came on; and frequently in the night walked mournfully about by myself, for I was a man of sorrows in the times of the first workings of the Lord in me.[5]

In Anglican tradition, faith is described as having three pillars: Scripture, reason and tradition. Revelations which come out of the desert come (paradoxical as it may sound) broadly under reason: that is, they come through the insight of individuals. But Scripture, tradition and reason all interact and help to test each other's insights.

We recognize that all divine communication and inspiration is mediated and communicated through people, so there is no Scripture, no tradition, and no reason that is reliable or authoritative beyond question. Revelations and ideas that come to one person are tested against Scripture and by the worshipping community before they are accepted. Traditions that grow up in one time and place are tested in others against Scripture and reason. Even Scriptures that are written at one time, in one place, and used in very different times and places, are tested against reason and tradition to see whether what they teach can still be accepted.

No one lives their whole life, or receives all their religious guidance, in solitary prayer. Almost all religious people emerge from a background in which Scripture and tradition are already present, and the insights we gain from solitary prayer are tested with reference to Scripture and by communities, and lived out in community. But communion with God which tries to leave behind our traditions and assumptions, and simply to wait on the presence and voice of God, is also an essential part of Christian life, and it may achieve insights that would not have been reached by the contemplative's staying within and accepting current tradition, practice and scriptural interpretation. To flourish, we need all three of the pillars of the faith.

Questions for discussion

- What factors make it easy or difficult to stay in touch with God in the course of everyday life?
- How (if at all) do you practise staying in touch?
- How does or might contemplation and/or prayer without ceasing affect your everyday activities?

7

Speaking of faith

Communicating the good news

'Preach the gospel at all times, and if necessary use words.'[1]
This well-known saying, derived from the Rule of St Francis, is
a good motto in any kind of ministry. If we practise ministering in everyday life, however – speaking and acting prophetically,
being open and attentive to the needs of others, living in love
and peace with our neighbours – then at some point people will
probably want to talk to us, about their own religious journey or
ours.

Being available to talk gives us an opportunity to share our faith
in a way which responds to the other person's needs and concerns.
To do that, we have to be attentive to the other person and their
perspective. It's important to respect people's existing convictions
and commitments, and to take up the discussion in a way that
makes sense to them.

When the Pentecost discussion group began to think about
ways of communicating our faith, some took the Franciscan
view that they would always prefer to act rather than to speak.
Others felt strongly that it was important to speak out. After
all, they said, the first apostles didn't rely on other kinds of ministry to make people notice them. They didn't wait for interested
enquirers to come to them, and they didn't leave those who did
to set the agenda. They preached the good news to convert their
listeners, without worrying about their perspective or respecting
their existing beliefs, and they told people that they must accept
it if they hoped to be saved.

This led us to look at some of the earliest stories of evangelism, in the Acts of the Apostles. What we found there was not quite what we'd expected. In Acts, some apostles do sometimes try to convert groups of people purely by preaching, but they usually fail. Paul, for instance, is repeatedly thrown out of the synagogues where he preaches, and when he preaches to Greeks in the theatre at Ephesus, he is nearly killed.

We noticed that when the disciples receive the Holy Spirit at Pentecost, the first thing that impresses the crowd around them is the miracle itself. The second is Peter's sermon, and the third, the 'many wonders and signs [which] were being done by the apostles' (2.43). Even when the apostles' audience consists of Jews and God-fearers, only part of the impact they make comes from preaching. When it includes Gentiles, preaching is usually less important still.

After Pentecost, the Jewish authorities warn the new apostles (Acts 4.18) not to proclaim the resurrection of Jesus from the dead. The way they pray, love and look after each other, however, continues to attract attention and new followers. People are amazed at the 'signs and wonders' Jesus' followers perform (5.12). The first deacon, Stephen, is 'full of grace and power', and works 'great wonders and signs among the people' (6.8). When Paul and Barnabas are imprisoned at Philippi (16.16–34), they are miraculously released by an earthquake, and their gaoler immediately asks how he can be saved. Throughout Acts, it is the example followers of Christ set, by their life of prayer and praise, their obvious love of God and one another, their care for the sick and vulnerable, and the visible, tangible power of the Spirit that runs through them, which most often convince people to follow Christ.

When preaching is most effective, it seems to be first, because the preacher has been invited to preach by his audience, second, because he has looked carefully at who the audience is, and third, because he is able to show them that his message fits to some degree with his audience's existing beliefs. When Philip encounters the Ethiopian God-fearer (6.26–39), for instance, he finds him reading Isaiah and uses the prophecy as his starting point, explaining that what it prophesies is the life and death of Jesus Christ. But the most striking example of an apostle's connecting with an audience through preaching is Paul's sermon in Athens, as reported by Luke (Acts 17.22–31).

Paul opens his Athenian mission, as usual, by preaching in the synagogue, but we do not hear whether he makes any converts. He also offers his views, in traditional Athenian style, for debate in the market place. A group of philosophers invite him to speak to them on the Areopagus hill.

Paul tells them that he knows the Athenians are deeply religious people. Then he says that the altar 'to an unknown god' which stands amid all the other altars in the centre of the city, is in fact an altar to his God, who is the God who made the world and everything in it. Throughout his speech, Paul emphasizes the closeness of his faith to that of the Athenians, describing God in terms familiar from Greek philosophy and religion, and quoting two sayings about the divine by Greek poets.

The discussion group was struck by how different this is from what most of us thought of as traditional evangelism. Paul plays down the uniqueness of his faith and emphasizes that what his audience already believes is largely right. Only at the very end of the speech does he offer them some new teaching (and he chooses just one aspect of the gospel with which to do it – perhaps the one he thinks they will find it easiest to understand). The good news of Jesus Christ, he says, is that judgement is near, so now is the time to repent of their sins. The concept of repentance already existed in Greek and Roman religion, as it did in Judaism, and so did the idea that the gods judge human action: it was the idea of imminent, universal judgement that was new. Acts tells us that some, at least, of the listeners were impressed by it and became believers (17.32–4).

In its sensitivity to other people's views, its respect for them, its willingness to explain the gospel in terms they already understand, and its interest in drawing parallels between Paul's own faith and other people's, this speech became a model for many other early

Christian writers. Here, for instance, is Justin Martyr (*c.*114–65) in his first Apology, which is addressed to the Roman emperor and his sons, explaining the similarities between Christianity and Graeco-Roman thought:

> ... [W]hen we say that all things have been created and arranged by God, we seem to express the doctrine of Plato; when we say that there will be a universal conflagration, we seem to express that of the Stoics; while we affirm that the souls of the unjust, which have feeling even after death, are punished, and that those of the good, released from punishment, live in blessedness, we seem to say the same things as the poets and philosophers; and when we say that people should not bow down before the works of their hands, we say the same things as have been said by the comic playwright Menander and others ...
>
> When we say that the Word, who is the first born of God, was created without sexual intercourse, and that He, Jesus Christ, our teacher, was crucified, died and rose again, and ascended into heaven, we say nothing stranger than what you say about those whom you call sons of Jupiter ...[2]

Over the centuries, some Christian writers have continued to try to explain their faith in ways that made sense to their immediate audiences. Others have drawn on ideas and images with universal appeal. Tertullian (*c.*160–*c.*225), for instance, explains the nature of the Trinity with a string of images drawn from nature.[3] God is like a plant, he says: a plant has a root, a shoot and a fruit, which all look different and have different functions, but they are all one plant. God is like the sun and its ray and the point of the ray: they share the same substance but they are different in form. God is like a fountain and the spring and river which flow from it.

The good news in the modern world

Our Pentecost group, like many Christians nowadays, held a wide range of views about other religious traditions. Some emphasized what is distinctive to Christianity; others were more strongly aware of what their faith has in common with other traditions. But we agreed that Christians have generally communicated the gospel most effectively when they have done two things. First, when they have visibly lived it themselves, and second, when they have engaged respectfully with those around them, making connections between their beliefs and other people's, and expressing what is distinctive about their faith in words their listeners can understand.

In recent history, this approach was exemplified by Bishop Pierre Claverie OP, who was Bishop of Oran in Algeria from 1981 to 1996. A profound believer in witness by example and in respectful engagement with those of other faiths, he spent much of his life trying to heal the damage done by French colonialism in Algeria, and encouraging dialogue between Christians and Muslims. He was assassinated by Muslim extremists in 1996 and is regarded as a modern martyr. This is an extract from his address at his installation as bishop:

Yes, our *church* is sent on a mission. I am not afraid to say this and to express my joy at entering with you in this mission. Many misunderstandings, which we have inherited, from history, bear on the mission and the missionaries. Let us state clearly today that:

We are not and do not want to be aggressors . . .

We are not and do not want to be the soldiers of a new crusade against Islam, against unbelief, or against anyone . . .

We do not wish to be the agents of an economic or cultural neo-colonialism that would divide the Algerian people the better to dominate them . . .

We are not nor do we wish to be among those evangelizers who think they are honouring the love of God through an indiscreet zeal or a total lack of respect for the culture, the faith of the other . . .

But we are and wish to be missionaries of the love of God, which we have discovered in Jesus Christ. This love, infinitely respectful of human beings, does not impose itself, does not impose anything, does not force consciences and hearts. With delicacy and solely through its presence, it liberates that which was in chains, reconciles that which was rent asunder, restores to its feet that which has been trodden down . . .

We recognize and believe in this love . . . It has possessed and swept us up. We believe that it can renew the life of humanity in so far as we acknowledge it.'[4]

To return to where we began this chapter, when we try to live a visibly Christian life, we may find people wanting to talk to us about our, or their faith. When that happens it helps, first of all, to develop a sense for what the other person really wants to discuss. If someone asks, 'What do you believe?' they may mean exactly that – or they may mean, 'What's the point of Christianity?' or, 'What should I believe?' If we listen attentively, and perhaps ask one or two gentle exploratory questions, we can usually work out which they mean.

Whatever we are being asked, it helps to be able to answer fairly briefly. This is harder than it sounds – partly because some of the central doctrines of Christianity, such as salvation by Christ, are not simple ideas, and partly because most of us do not have much experience in expressing what we believe.

During my ordination training, I was often asked why I was hoping to be ordained. I didn't have a short, pithy answer, and when I tried to explain at length, I invariably found that people stopped listening before the end of the first sentence. Eventually, I realized that most people weren't interested in my spiritual journey. What they were really asking was, 'What do you believe?' or, 'What's the point of being a Christian?' and what they wanted was a short, clear answer. I never did work out a short clear answer at the time. But I did begin to ponder seriously how to explain my faith, especially to someone who did not share it.

One reason why most of us find it hard to explain our faith, especially if we were born into our tradition, is simply that we have never needed to. Usually, we express it rather than articulate it, by going to church, saying our prayers and loving God and our neighbours. If we did make a habit of describing it, parts of our description might well evolve from year to year. About some questions, we might never be absolutely certain what we believed.

If describing faith isn't easy, we can all get better at it with practice. But before we begin, it is worth thinking a little about the meaning of faith itself: what we mean when we say that we 'have faith' or 'believe in God'.

The meaning of faith

Christians talk about faith and belief more than people of any other religion. We are encouraged to *have faith*, and we regularly say the creeds, which begin, 'I believe . . .' or 'We believe in one God'. And Christians are often criticized for 'believing impossible things', like the virgin birth or the physical resurrection.

The idea that faith is the basis of the relationship between God and humanity has its roots in the Hebrew Bible, though it never becomes central to Judaism as it does to Christianity. The Hebrew words which Christians translate with the language of 'faith' or 'belief' mean variously 'to nurture', 'to take refuge in', 'to have confidence in', 'to trust'; 'steadfast', 'reliable' or 'loyal'. When the Hebrew Bible talks about someone 'having faith' or 'keeping faith', they usually mean that the person is trustworthy or faithful. Faith is a relationship, and both human beings and God can be faithful. God is loyal and trustworthy towards Israel, and asks the Israelites to be the same towards him.

Two characters in the Old Testament were seen as models of faith – Abraham and King David. Abraham put his trust in God when God called him, at the age of 75, to leave his homeland and move to another land. He trusted God again when God told him that he and his elderly wife, Sarai, would have a son. He remained loyal to God all his life, even when God told him to sacrifice the son whom God had given him.

David too trusted God, and let God work through him to make Israel great. In both men, trusting God led to obeying God and letting themselves be used by God, and those qualities also became part of faith.

The other characters in the Hebrew Bible who are famous for their faith are the prophets. Prophets too trust and obey God and let God use them, and they add another dimension to faith: hope. They are usually called when Israel is in trouble, and by their hopeful faithfulness they help Israel change for the better.

In the New Testament, the Greek word *pistis*, which is usually translated as 'faith' or 'belief', and its relatives, also mean 'trust', 'trustworthy', 'reliable' and 'loyal'. Christians add yet more dimensions to faith. When Jesus says, 'Repent, and believe in the good news' (Mark 1.15), 'believing' means turning to God and away from your bad ways. That moment of conversion to God, the act of putting your trust in God, becomes part of faith. Sometimes, too, in the New Testament, 'faith' or 'belief' seems to mean belief not in a person or a relationship, but in an idea. When St Paul says (Rom. 10.9), 'If you confess with your lips that Jesus is Lord and believe in your heart that God raised him from the dead, you will be saved', he says not only that we should trust Jesus but that we should believe certain things about him.

This type of faith is often called 'propositional belief' (propositional beliefs are statements like, 'I believe the earth is round' and, 'I believe the sun will rise tomorrow'). This is the kind of belief non-Christians often find hardest to understand. People wonder how Christians can believe in apparently bizarre things, like miracles, or heaven and hell.

We have slipped in the last few lines from talking about 'faith' to talking about 'belief', and this slip is significant. English is unusual in having two words, faith and belief, where most languages have only one. Nowadays we tend to use 'belief' particularly to mean 'propositional belief', but in the past, the distinction between 'faith' and 'belief' was much less strong. This development in language sometimes leads us, when we read older texts, to misunderstand their meaning.

When the word 'believe' first appears in English in the Middle Ages, it has two forms, 'believe' and 'belove', which have the same meaning: 'to hold dear', 'to prize' or 'to give your heart to' some-thing. Over time, 'believe' gradually changed from meaning 'to give your heart' to 'to take something to heart', 'to accept', 'to trust' or 'have faith in'. (We still use it that way. If I say, 'I believe in you', I don't mean I think I can prove you exist; I mean that I have confidence in you.) Finally, belief also came to mean 'to know' or 'to think that something is so'.

When, at the Reformation, the first Anglicans translated the creed into English as, 'We believe in God', they did not mean, 'We think it is a fact that God exists.' They took it for granted that God exists, and intended the creed to mean, 'We put our trust and hope in God.'

It seems that even at the time, some people were confused and thought that the creed was making a propositional statement, so Archbishop Cranmer wrote a sermon about faith which was to be read out in churches throughout the country. In this sermon, he explains that although propositional belief is part of Christianity, it is not the most important part. Faith is above all about putting one's trust in God, having confidence and hope in God, obeying God and doing God's work of love.

> Even the devils know and believe, that Christ was born of a virgin, that he fasted forty days and forty nights, without meat and drink, that he wrought all kind of miracles, declar-ing himself very God. They believe also that Christ, for our sakes, suffered most painful death, to redeem us from eternal death, and that he rose again from death, the third day; they believe that he ascended into heaven, and that he sitteth on the right hand of the Father, and that at the last end of this world, shall come again and judge both the quick and the dead. These articles of our faith the devils believe . . . and yet for all this faith, they be but devils, remaining still in their damnable estate, lacking the very true Christian faith. For the right and true Christian faith, is not only to believe that holy Scripture, and all the foresaid articles of our faith are true, but also to have a sure trust and confidence, in God's

merciful promises, to be saved from everlasting damnation, by Christ; whereof doth follow a loving heart, to obey his commandments.[5]

Propositional belief is part of faith. If you give your heart to anything, you must think or trust or hope (or all three) that it is real. If you put your faith in another being, you believe there is reason to do so. But when we say that we believe in miracles or the resurrection, we don't mean that we think we can prove them. We mean that because we have confidence in what we have heard and experienced of God and Christ, we are prepared to take on trust things that have been revealed and reported about them. At the same time, we accept that God remains a mystery, so anything we say about God's actions must always be provisional, poetic and intuitive.[6]

Some of the things which faith asks us to take on trust are extraordinary. We may find them very hard to understand or accept. But our sense of God includes the sense that there are things about the divine which we do not understand, and may never understand, and have to take on trust. It is a risk. Putting one's faith in anyone or anything is always a risk.

The idea that faith is strongly relational fits with the idea we have explored in earlier chapters, that the heart of Christian life is our relationship with God. When we describe God as a loving, faithful, caring being – when we call God father or mother and other human beings sisters and brothers – then we are placing a relationship at the centre of our faith.

In 1 Corinthians 13, St Paul links faith with hope and love, and when we reflect on all the things that faith involves – trust, obedience and loyalty; turning away from this world towards the mysterious other – we can see why love and hope are inextricably involved with it. No one puts their trust in something without giving something of themselves to it. No one takes a risk without hope. No one gives their life to another being without both hope and love.

As in any relationship, the truth of our relationship with God can be seen in the quality of the relationship itself. If we flourish in it and are healed, transformed and fulfilled – if the joy of it radiates out from us to touch the people that we meet and makes them flourish too – then we can have confidence that it is a good relationship. So Paul ends 1 Corinthians 13 by telling us that of faith, hope and love, the greatest is not faith, but love. If we have love, then we are faithful. If we have love, then God's faithfulness can work through us. If we have love, then, as Paul says, 'all things work together for good' in us (Rom. 8.28). This is more than anything what we hope for in our faith.

Speaking of faith

Our Pentecost group all agreed that we found it difficult to describe or explain our own faith. We decided to make a start by each choosing one or two verses from the Bible which summed up something of our faith. Even this turned out to be harder than we expected – in fact, the first time we tried to do it, only Ray could come up with a verse on the spur of the moment. The rest of us decided we needed a week to think about it. The following week, each of us came back with a verse or two. Below are some of the most popular:

'Ask, and it will be given to you; search, and you will find; knock, and the door will be opened for you.' (Matt. 7.7)

'Come to me, all you that are weary and are carrying heavy burdens, and I will give you rest.' (Matt. 11.28)

'Let it be it with me according to your word.' (Luke 1.38)

'For God so loved the world that he gave his only Son, so that everyone who believes in him may not perish but may have eternal life.' (John 3.16)

I have been crucified with Christ; and it is no longer I who live, but it is Christ who lives in me. (Gal. 2.19–20)

God is love, and those who abide in love abide in God, and God abides in them. (1 John 4.16)

The LORD is my shepherd; I shall not want. (Ps. 23.1)

We did not expect these few verses to produce a complete picture of our faith, but we were surprised by how much they did tell us.

One theme which runs through several of them is that God loves us, looks after us, and wants to welcome us into eternal life. Another is that if we look for God, we will find God. Behind both these ideas lies the conviction that God is the highest power of the universe, who not only wants to bring us to eternal life, but is able to do so.

Another theme to be found here is that God, or Christ, is in us and works through us. Linked with this is the idea of self-dedication: the belief that we put ourselves into God's hands to do God's will.

1 John tells us that God is love, but statements about God's nature play rather a small part in the verses above. Several, though, focus on our relationship with God. Some of them are addressed to the reader or listener, to encourage and reassure us. In some, we speak to God, to dedicate ourselves to God.

Some of the verses spoke more strongly to some people than others, but between them, we felt, they captured quite a lot of what is central to our faith. God is the power at the heart of all things. God loves us, wants to welcome us to Godself and, through Christ, makes Godself available to us when we seek God. We long to give our love, our obedience and our lives to God, letting Christ work through us and do as God wishes with our lives. We trust that by doing this, not only we, but ultimately the whole world, will be united in God's love.

Another way that our Pentecost group practised describing our faith was by reading and discussing the Lord's Prayer. The Lord's Prayer (Matt. 6.9–13; Luke 11.2–4) is not only the first and most important Christian prayer; it also tells us a good deal about Christian faith. It expresses many of the same ideas as the verses above (below is my translation of Matthew's version):

> Our Father in the heavens,
> may your name be sanctified,
> may your reign come,

> may your will be done
> on earth as in heaven;
> give us today the bread of life,
> and release us from our debts
> as we release our debtors;
> and do not put us to the test,
> but deliver us from evil.

When we say, 'Our Father in the heavens, may your name be sanctified, may your reign come', we affirm that God is the highest power of the universe. We are made in God's image, and God loves us and cares for us as our father. We want everyone to be moved, as we are, to praise God. We look forward to the time when we and all people put ourselves wholly in God's hands.

'Give us today the bread of life' expresses our confidence that God looks after us. The word which we often translate 'daily', and I have translated 'of life', has not been found anywhere else in Greek. As a result, we are not sure exactly what it means: our best guess is that it means either 'ordinary, everyday bread' or 'the food of eternal life'. In the Gospels, Jesus encourages us to rely on God both for everyday life and for eternal life, so we probably will not be far wrong if we take 'bread of life' to mean both.

'Release us from our debts, as we release our debtors', which can also be translated, 'Forgive us our sins, as we forgive those who sin against us', expresses our sense that our relationships with God and one another are not as they should be. Too often, we have wasted God's gifts to us and our gifts to each other; we have turned away from God, and damage each other by our failures in love. But we have confidence that God wants us to be reunited with God and to help us be reconciled with one another.[7]

'Do not lead us into temptation' or 'Do not put us to the test', 'but deliver us from evil', is another phrase whose meaning is not certain. To the Pentecost group it said that we know we are fragile, imperfect beings, who find it hard to withstand the trials of daily life and our own unhelpful passions. We need God's help to be faithful. We remember that even Jesus, in the garden of

Gethsemane, asked not to be put to the test. Recognizing that we need help, helps to guard against the temptations of pride or overconfidence, and reminds us daily to keep turning to God for strength.

The earliest manuscripts of the Gospels do not include the doxology, 'For the kingdom, the power and the glory are yours, now and forever', and nowadays we say the prayer both with and without it. The doxology (which is based on 1 Chronicles 29.11–13) expresses again both our trust in God's power and glory, and that we joyfully give our lives to God; and we end with the affirmative, 'Amen', 'so be it'. The whole prayer captures the joy, trust, obedience and hope which are central to our relationship with God, and every time we say it, it reminds us how to be faithful.

In another session, the Pentecost group spent a long time discussing the passage which is partly quoted below, from Paul's Letter to the Romans (5.1–2, 6–8). This is one of Paul's most sustained attempts to express what he believes about God and Christ and what it means to follow Christ, and long before the first official Creeds were written, it is effectively a credal statement:

> Therefore, since we are justified by faith, we have peace with God through our Lord Jesus Christ, through whom we have obtained access to this grace in which we stand; and we boast in our hope of sharing the glory of God ... For while we were still weak, at the right time Christ died for the ungodly. Indeed, rarely will anyone die for a righteous person – though perhaps for a good person someone might actually dare to die. But God proves his love for us in that while we were still sinners Christ died for us.   (5.1–2, 6–8)

The word often translated 'justified' means 'made just', 'made righteous' or 'made right with God'. For Paul, the death and resurrection of Christ somehow release human beings from the trap of sin in which they have been caught since Adam's disobedience to God, and restore them to the way they were meant to be. God sent Christ, and Christ died for us because God loves us, and we have only to respond to that love to have everything to celebrate and

124

to hope for. The group didn't find this an easy passage to get to grips with, but we agreed that it was worth more reflection.

The Bible is full of passages which express various aspects of our belief, and as we read and hear it, it is always worth asking which passages speak to us most clearly, and why. These passages also make a good focus for contemplative prayer. The Pentecost group, though, felt strongly that if we wanted to be able to communicate our faith, we needed to do more than reflect on the words of the Bible. We had to try to express our beliefs in language which our families and friends could understand, even if they had little or no experience of Christianity.

Speaking of faith today

Early Christian doctrine was developed in the Near East and Europe, using languages and ideas native to those cultures and intellectual traditions. Christian missionaries have always found themselves adjusting their language to make sense to the people they lived among – like the nineteenth-century missionary to the Inuit who, in a society without sheep, took to describing Christ as the 'baby seal of God'. In recent years, theologians from Africa, South America and the Far East, along with feminist theologians from many countries, have led the way in looking for re-expressions of Christian doctrine which make sense to people from very different cultures and societies.

In the introduction to his book *Waterbuffalo Theology*, the Japanese theologian Kosuke Koyama explains how he came to realize the importance of describing Christian faith in language which relatively uneducated Christians in Thailand (where he was working at the time) would understand:

> On my way to the country church, I never fail to see a herd of waterbuffaloes grazing in the muddy paddy field. This sight is an inspiring moment for me. Why? Because it reminds me that the people to whom I am to bring the gospel of Christ spend most of their time with these waterbuffaloes in the rice

125

field. The waterbuffaloes tell me that I must preach to these farmers in the simplest sentence-structure and thought-development. They remind me to discard all abstract ideas, and to use exclusively objects that are immediately tangible. 'Sticky-rice', 'banana', 'pepper', 'dog', 'cat', 'bicycle', 'rainy season', 'leaking house', 'fishing', 'cock-fighting', 'lottery', 'stomach ache' – these are meaningful words for them. 'This morning,' I say to myself, 'I will try to bring the gospel of Christ through the medium of cock-fighting!'[8]

Vincent Donovan met the same challenge while acting as a missionary to the Masai of Tanzania. In *Christianity Rediscovered*, he describes some of the ways he tried to express the good news so that it would make sense to his Masai friends. Like St Paul among the Athenians, he began by stressing his respect for their culture, and what he believed Christians and the Masai already shared:

I told them I believed that they knew about God long before we came, and that they were a devout and very pious people in the face of God. It was not our belief that God loved us Christians more than them, nor that God had abandoned them or forgotten them until we came along. From the beginning it was evident that we were going to have to learn from them as well as teach them.[9]

Donovan retold Bible stories using local language and ideas. Pharisees became witch doctors; the Temple in Jerusalem became the local sacred mountain. He also encouraged Masai to find their own ways of expressing what he was teaching them. Together, they evolved the summary of Masai Christian faith which appears with some other creeds and confessions in the appendix.

Koyama and Donovan both aimed to teach traditional doctrine in fresh languages. Other theologians have found that taking their faith into a new environment, or sharing it with a particular group of people, has challenged their understanding of what the gospel is.

Desmond Tutu grew up in South Africa but received much of his theological education in England, where he trained for the priesthood. When he returned to Africa, he found that the language of faith he had been taught did not begin to meet the suffering of black people under apartheid. 'How do you speak about a God who loves you, a redeemer, a saviour, when you live like an animal? . . . [T]he third world must develop its own [theological] style geared to its own needs and maybe we could still teach others a thing or two.'[10]

In an unpublished paper from 1974, Tutu describes what he means in more detail:

> Black theology has to do with whether it is possible to be black and continue to be Christian; it is to ask on whose side is God; it is to be concerned about the humanisation of man, because those who ravage our humanity dehumanise them-selves in the process; [it says] that the liberation of the black man is the other side of the coin of the liberation of the white man – so it is concerned with human liberation. It is a clarion call for man to align himself with the God who is the God of the Exodus, God the liberator, who leads his people, all his people, out of all kinds of bondage – political, economic, cultural, the bondage of sin and disease, into the glorious liberty of the sons of God.[11]

Even in Europe, modern Christians often feel the need to rethink the religious language they have inherited. In his 2004 book, *Quantum Theology: Spiritual Implications of the New Physics*, the Irish theologian Diarmuid O'Murchu reformulated traditional doctrine for a modern Western audience using the language of quantum physics.

'Quantum theology', says O'Murchu, teaches us to see everything that exists as a unity, and God as being in every part of it, forming a creative, self-regulating whole which is constantly in harmonious motion, perpetually changing as parts of it come into being and disappear. Creation is a web of relationships whose elements, like particles and waves, are both discrete and inseparable.

O'Murchu's description of the relationship between God and the world encourages us, he says, to think in new ways about that relationship. Quantum theology invites us to think, not only about the relationship of human beings with God, but about both God's and our relationships with all creation. It allows us to think of God, not as separate from the world, but as present in all aspects of creation. And it encourages us not only to speak of God in anthropomorphic terms, but also to look for other ways of expressing the divine nature.[12]

Feminist theology arose in many parts of the world at roughly the same time in the mid-twentieth century, as theologians who were women began to point out that the very male-dominated language of much Christian teaching did not speak to them. Worse, such language has often been used to justify institutions and social practices which are controlled by men and degrade women. Feminist theologians began to recover images, stories and ideas in the Bible and in Christian tradition which affirm the feminine in God and creation and speak to followers of Christ as women.

In the Bible, for instance, God is sometimes described using feminine language. God is like a woman in labour (Isa. 42.14), or a mother who suckles her children or comforts them.[13] God makes clothes (Neh. 9.21) and bread (Luke 13.18–21) like a woman, and in the parable of the lost coin, God is the woman looking for her coin (Luke 15.8–10). God is described several times as a mother bird, protecting her young under or on her wings.[14] In both Old and New Testaments, women also play essential parts, from Sarah, Miriam, Hannah and Esther to Elizabeth, Mary, Jesus' female disciples in the Gospels and the female co-workers and deacons in Paul's letters.

In her book *Compassionate and Free*, the Indonesian theologian Marianne Katoppo describes how she persuaded a (male) colleague that the God of the Bible is both masculine and feminine:

A professor at a theological seminary in Indonesia once said to me in all seriousness: 'Well, you can't deny it –

God is male: just look at the way he is referred to as "he" throughout the Bible, with all the masculine forms of the verbs and nouns!' . . .

I asked him about the original meaning of *rechamim*, which is used for God's mercy, compassion (e.g. Exod. 34). He admitted that it literally means 'movements of the womb' (*rechem*).

Neither of us knew of any males who possessed wombs, so my professor was persuaded there might be a touch of the feminine here . . .

I also asked how women could have been created in God's image if God was so decidedly male. And I pointed to the case of the Holy Spirit. The Third Person [of the Trinity] started out in Hebrew as the feminine *Ruach*, but then was effectively neutered by the Greek translators of the Septuagint [because the Greek for 'spirit', *pneuma*, is neuter], then made masculine by Latin [*spiritus*].[15]

Katoppo goes on to point out that the name of God, YHWH, in Hebrew, is not a noun, and is grammatically neither male nor female, but probably derives from the verb 'to be' or 'to become'.

These examples remind us of an important point about Christian teaching. Two thousand years of teaching, practice, Bible study, prayer, thought, inspiration and experience have created in Christianity a very rich, complex and diverse tradition. Christians across time and throughout the world share much, but they can also take very different views about many things, including how to interpret the Bible and how to understand the nature of God, or Christ, or God's actions in the world. Even within one church congregation or study group, we often find, if people start talking about what they believe, a remarkably wide range of views.

Individuals and communities need to find a balance between what the Bible and tradition tells them is the heart of the gospel, and what speaks to their condition in the world they live in. The most powerful elements of the gospel are those which have spoken to us in the past, and still speak now.

When we as individuals give thought to what we believe, and practise expressing it, we need to keep this same balance in mind. Christianity is not a private religion; we can't believe anything we like and still be part of the wider community. On the other hand, faith deals with profound mysteries: no one has ever seen God and no one can be certain that they know the whole truth about humanity's relationship with God. There is room within the community for quite a wide range of understandings, and understanding (we hope) grows with every generation. So when we try to articulate our faith, we need to test it constantly against what we find in the Bible, what we have been taught and what those around us believe – but we need not be afraid to try.

Finding our own words

Our Pentecost discussion group found expressing our faith in words that modern, non-churchgoing people in Littlemore and Sandford might understand, the hardest thing we did together. But we have gone on thinking about it ever since, and also about the slightly different languages we might need to use to talk, for instance, to friends or neighbours or colleagues. Our starting points are questions like: What do I give my heart to? What does my community trust and have confidence in? What do we hope to express in our lives, our words and actions?

The Appendix gives just a few examples of the many statements of faith which Christian individuals and communities have evolved over the years. They have much in common, and are also different in many ways. It is not the job of this book to tell readers how to express their own faith. But to end, I offer one example of one way I might try to explain something of my own faith to someone from a similar background, but who was not a practising Christian. Like any creed, this doesn't capture everything I would like to say, nor how I would say it in every context, but it's a start.

I believe that everything that is, is one, a unity which is fundamentally harmonious. Our experience of this harmony is what we call good, and this good and harmonious unity is what we call God. Everything that exists, is part of God.

Within the unity of all things, there is an infinite plurality of energies and elements, which endlessly evolve, diversify and recombine. Because creation is plural as well as one, these elements can come into conflict with one another, compete, attack and damage one another. I believe that God both rejoices in the diversity of creation and takes every opportunity to reconcile creation with itself; to heal the damage it does to itself. This desire, and the work it does, is love, and when we share it, we love as God loves us.

I believe that Jesus Christ was, and is, both part of creation and wholly divine. As part of creation, he experienced to the full the imperfections of our world. As God, he was not damaged by them. He looked deeply into people, seeing both how they were damaged and also the seeds of trust, hope and love within them. He responded to their damage with love, helping them to heal and to be reconciled with one another. By his death, and appearances to his followers after his death, he showed that even death cannot destroy such love. Jesus showed his followers that having been touched and changed by him, they carried him in their hearts, minds, bodies and souls, and could continue his work of love and pass it on to others.

I believe that the Spirit of God continues to work throughout creation. Followers of Jesus Christ open themselves to its creative power, asking for healing for themselves and for all beings.

I put my trust in God: in unity, in meaning and in love. I put my trust in Jesus Christ, who shows us how to be human and how to be one with God. I put my trust in the Spirit of God, which gives life to the world.

Faith is the sense that there is more to life than meets the eye. It is the echo in creation of something greater than itself – the persistent conviction that the life which runs through us is more than our own. It is the experience that we live more fully when we let this greater life flow freely through us and direct our living. It is a movement of the heart – from giving our hearts to the material here and now, to putting our trust and hope in that mysterious other which is the source and fulfilment of all being. Amen.

Questions for discussion

- Which passage(s) from the Bible capture something of the essence of your faith, and why?
- What do you most want to say about your faith to someone who knows little or nothing about Christianity?
- What do you think it is not particularly important to say about your faith to someone who knows little or nothing about Christianity? Why?

Conclusion

Three years have passed since the Sandford and Littlemore Pentecost discussion group first met. Two of our members have died and one has moved away. The rest of us continue to live and work locally and to worship in our respective churches.

Our lives have not changed dramatically, but they have evolved. We have gone on thinking, individually and together, about the topics we discussed. We have gone on trying to put our reflections into practice.

Some of us are engaged in fresh prophetic action. Sue has founded Littlemore's first café (staffed by volunteers), and Shirley is helping to create new activities for over-50s. We're teaching the basics of Christianity in the local secondary school using contemporary slogans and catchphrases as starting points ('Why should I?' 'Everybody else does.' 'Because I'm worth it.' 'Whatever.'). We continue to try to love and be attentive to our neighbours. We meet regularly to talk about tackling unhelpful passions or the meaning of faith, and we have gone on taking contemplative prayer to work.

We have all come to believe more and more strongly that every Christian is called to be an apostle. We are all sent out to minister in all the places where we live and work.

We don't think you have to be a hero to be an apostle. You don't have to be holy. You just have to be prepared to hear a call and go where it sends you.

Whatever gifts you have can be well used. Whatever time you have can be well spent. Wherever you spend your time, you can make a difference, to individuals and communities and institutions.

There is no one better to do it than you. Not only does Christ have no other hands or feet on earth but yours – he has no better. Because nothing touches a human heart like another human heart.

Nothing shows the presence of God with us more clearly than the presence among us of people who love and serve God with all their heart and soul and mind and strength.

Where is God sending you? How will you minister?

Appendix:
some statements of faith

—•◆•—

These pre-credal and credal statements (just a tiny selection of the scores of creeds which have been written in different times and places) emphasize different aspects of faith, depending on their original author, purpose and audience. Some are particularly concerned with the nature of God, Christ and the Spirit, others with what they do. Some are only concerned with God, while others range widely over such topics as angels, the soul, the Bible, human behaviour, original sin, the nature and operation of the Church, public worship, civil government, or challenges facing Christians of the day.

St Paul, 1 Corinthians 15.3–8

For I handed on to you as of first importance what I in turn had received: that Christ died for our sins in accordance with the scriptures, and that he was buried, and that he was raised on the third day in accordance with the scriptures, and that he appeared to Cephas, then to the twelve. Then he appeared to more than five hundred brothers and sisters at one time, most of whom are still alive, though some have died. Then he appeared to James, then to all the apostles. Last of all, as to one untimely born, he appeared also to me.

Irenaeus, *Against Heresies* 1.10.1

Born in Asia Minor in about AD 130, Irenaeus became Bishop of Lyons in Southern France, and is thought to have been martyred in about 200. A prolific writer, he is regarded as the first great theologian of Western Christianity.

The Church ... has received from both the apostles and their followers this faith, which is in one God, Father almighty, who made heaven and earth and the sea and everything which is in them; and in one Christ Jesus the Son of God, who became flesh for our salvation; and in the Holy Spirit, who announced the dispositions of God and the coming [of Christ] and that birth from a Virgin and the passion and resurrection from the dead and ascension in the flesh into heaven of the beloved Jesus Christ, our Lord, and his coming from heaven in the glory of the Father to gather everything into one and to raise all human flesh from the dead, so that every knee in heaven and earth and hell should bend to Jesus Christ our Lord, God, Saviour and King in accordance with the will of the Father, and every tongue should confess him, and so that he should pass just judgement on everybody . . .

Tertullian, *Against Heretics* 13: the 'rule of faith'

Tertullian was born in Carthage in about AD 160 and lived all his life in North Africa. He was trained as a lawyer and is most famous for highly polemical works against pagans and heretics. He wrote prolifically and had a great influence on Western Christianity.

There is only one God, who is none other than the creator of the world who produced everything out of nothing by his word, which was sent out before anything. This word is called his Son, which under the name of God was seen in various ways by the patriarchs, heard constantly in the prophets, and finally was brought down by the Spirit and power of God the Father into the virgin Mary, made flesh in her womb and was born of her as Jesus Christ. From there he preached the new Law and the new promise of the kingdom of heaven; he performed miracles, was crucified, rose on the third day, was taken into the heavens, and sits at the right hand of the Father. He sent in his place the power of the Holy Spirit who guides the faithful, and he will come again with glory to take the holy to the enjoyment of everlasting life and the promised heavenly joys, and to consign the wicked to perpetual fire, after the resurrection of both groups has occurred in the flesh. This rule, as will be shown, was taught by Christ, and prompts no questions among us except those which heresies introduce and which make heretics.

Origen, *On First Principles* pr. 4

A native of Alexandria in Egypt, Origen lived from c. AD 185–254 and taught widely around the Mediterranean. He was one of the early Church's most creative thinkers: an equally remarkable theologian, biblical interpreter and writer on spirituality.

These are the things which are clearly handed down through the preaching of the apostles. First, that there is one God, who created and arranged everything, and who, when nothing existed, made everything exist, God from the first creation and foundation of the world, God of all the just: Adam, Abel, Seth, Enos, Enoch, Noe, Sem, Abraham, Isaac, Jacob, the twelve patriarchs, Moses and the prophets. This God, in the latter days, as he had previously promised through his prophets, sent the Lord Jesus Christ, first to call Israel, then indeed even the gentiles after the betrayal of the people of Israel. This just and good God, Father of our Lord Jesus Christ, who is God alike of the apostles and of the Old and New Testaments, himself gave us the Law and prophets and gospels.

Secondly, that Christ Jesus, the one who came, was born of the Father before all creation. When he had served the Father in the foundation of all things, for, 'through him all things were made', he recently stripped himself of his glory and was made man, was made flesh, even though he was God, and being made man he remained what he was, God. He put on a body like our body, differing only in that it was born of a virgin and the Holy Spirit. And because this Jesus Christ was truly born, he truly suffered, and truly, not just in appearance, died the common death; and he truly rose from the dead and after his resurrection he spoke with his disciples and was taken up to heaven.

Ambrose of Milan, *On the Sacraments* 2.7.20

Ambrose (c. AD 339–97) was brought up in a Christian family but pursued a political career and was not baptized until he was unexpectedly made Bishop of Milan in 374. He became a famous preacher, a successful Church politician, and was partly responsible

*for the conversion of St Augustine. Here he describes the questions
a candidate answers at baptism.*

You were asked, 'Do you believe in God the Father almighty?' You
said, 'I believe,' and you were immersed – that is, you were buried.
Then you were asked, 'Do you believe in our Lord Jesus Christ
and in his cross?' You said, 'I believe,' and were immersed. So you
were buried with Christ, for the one who is buried with Christ
rises again with Christ. Thirdly you were asked, 'Do you also believe
in the Holy Spirit?' You said, 'I believe,' and you were immersed a
third time so that your threefold confession absolved you from
the many failings of your previous life.

John Henry Newman (1801–90), 'Firmly I believe and truly'

Firmly I believe and truly
God is three and God is One;
and I next acknowledge duly
manhood taken by the Son.

And I trust and hope most fully
in that manhood crucified;
and each thought and deed unruly
do to death as he has died.

Simply to his grace and wholly
light and life and strength belong,
and I love supremely, solely,
him the holy, him the strong.

And I hold in veneration,
for the love of him alone,
holy Church as his creation,
and her teachings as his own.

Adoration ay be given,
with and through th' angelic host,

to the God of earth and heaven,
Father, Son and Holy Ghost.

John Donne (1571–1631), Sonnet

Wilt thou love God, as he thee? then digest
My Soul, this wholesome meditation,
How God the Spirit, by Angels waited on
In heaven, doth make his Temple in thy breast.
The Father having begot a Son most blest,
And still begetting, (for he ne'er begonne)
Hath deign'd to choose thee by adoption,
Coheir to his glory, and Sabbath's endlesse rest;
And, as a robbed man, which by search doth find
His stolen stuff sold, must lose or buy it again:
The Son of glory came down, and was slain,
Us whom he had made, and Satan stole, to unbind.
'Twas much, that man was made like God before,
But, that God should be made like man, much more.

The Scots' Confession, 1560

This confession of faith was written under the leadership of John Knox, at the direction of the Scottish parliament, and was ratified in parliament; it made Scotland legally a Protestant state. After these first two articles, it goes on to talk about original sin, the nature of Christ and salvation, the nature and working of the Church, predestination, good works, the soul, doctrine, the authority of the Scriptures and the sacraments.

We confess and acknowledge one God alone, to whom alone we must cleave, whom alone we must serve, whom alone we must worship, and in whom alone we put our trust; who is eternal, infinite, immeasurable, incomprehensible, omnipotent, invisible; one in substance and yet distinct in three persons; the Father, the Son, and the Holy Spirit; by whom we confess and believe all things in heaven and earth, visible and invisible, to have been created, to be retained in their being, and to be ruled and guided by his inscrutable providence for such end as his eternal wisdom, goodness, and justice have appointed, and to the manifestation of his own glory.

We confess and acknowledge that God has created man, to wit our first father, Adam, after his own image and likeness, to whom he gave wisdom, lordship, justice, free will, and self-consciousness, so that in the whole nature of man no imperfection could be found. From this dignity and perfection man and woman both fell; the woman being deceived by the serpent and man obeying the voice of the woman, both conspiring against the sovereign majesty of God, who in clear words had previously threatened death if they presumed to eat of the forbidden fruit . . .

A Masai Creed (V. Donovan, *Christianity Rediscovered*, p. 200)

We believe in the one High God who out of love created the beautiful world and everything good in it. He created man and wanted man to be happy in the world. God loves the world and every nation and tribe on the earth. We have known this High God in the darkness, and now we know him in the light. God promised in the book of his word, the Bible, that he would save the world and all the nations and tribes.

We believe that God made good his promise by sending his son, Jesus Christ, a man in the flesh, a Jew by tribe, born poor in a little village, who left his home and was always on safari doing good, curing people by the power of God, teaching about God and man, showing that the meaning of religion is love. He was rejected by his people, tortured and nailed hands and feet to a cross, and died. He lay buried in the grave, but the hyenas did not touch him, and on the third day, he rose from the grave. He ascended to the skies. He is the Lord.

We believe that all our sins are forgiven through him. All who have faith in him must be sorry for their sins, be baptized in the Holy Spirit of God, live the rules of love and share the bread together in love, to announce the good news to others until Jesus comes again. We are waiting for him. He is alive. He lives. This we believe. Amen.

The Lausanne Covenant, 1974

This covenant was drawn up as an agreed statement of faith for Catholic and Protestant evangelicals who participated in the First International Congress of Evangelicals. After these first two articles, it goes on to talk about Christ, evangelism, social responsibility, the Church, education and leadership, spiritual conflict, freedom and persecution, the power of the Holy Spirit and the return of Christ.

We affirm our belief in the one eternal God, creator and lord of the world, Father, Son and Holy Spirit, who governs all things according to the purpose of his will. He has been calling out from the world a people for himself, and sending his people back into the world to be his servants and his witnesses, for the extension of his kingdom, the building up of Christ's body, and the glory of his name. We confess with shame that we have often denied our calling and failed in our mission, by becoming conformed to the world or by withdrawing from it. Yet we rejoice that even when borne by earthen vessels the gospel is still a precious treasure. To the task of making that treasure known in the power of the Holy Spirit we desire to dedicate ourselves anew.

We affirm the divine inspiration, truthfulness and authority of both Old and New Testament Scriptures in their entirety as the only written word of God, without error in all that it affirms, and the only infallible rule of faith and practice. We also affirm the power of God's word to accomplish his purpose of salvation. The message of the Bible is addressed to all men and women. For God's revelation in Christ and in Scripture is unchangeable. Through it the Holy Spirit still speaks today. He illumines the minds of God's people in every culture to perceive its truth freshly through their own eyes and thus discloses to the whole Church ever more of the many-colored wisdom of God . . .

**Authorized affirmations of faith from *Common Worship*,
pp. 147, 148.**

Let us affirm our faith in Jesus Christ the Son of God.
Though he was divine,
he did not cling to equality with God,
but made himself nothing.
Taking the form of a slave,
he was born in human likeness.
He humbled himself
and was obedient to the death,
even the death of the cross.
Therefore God has raised him on high,
and given him the name above every name:
that at the name of Jesus
every knee should bow,
and every voice proclaim that Jesus Christ is Lord,
to the glory of God the Father. Amen.   (cf. Phil. 2.6–11)

We believe in God the Father,
from whom every family
in heaven and on earth is named.

We believe in God the Son,
who lives in our hearts through faith,
and fills us with his love.

We believe in God the Holy Spirit,
who strengthens us
with power from on high.

We believe in one God;
Father, Son and Holy Spirit. Amen.   (cf. Eph. 3)

Notes

Introduction: ministry for all believers

1 Mark 3.14, 6.30; Matt. 10.2, 10.16; Luke e.g. 6.13.
2 Paul himself describes being an apostle as one form of ministry among many: 1 Cor. 12.28–29.
3 10.16; cf. Luke 10.1–3.
4 Cf. Luke 10.27; Mark 22.37–39; Matt. 12.29–31.
5 Mark 10.21; cf. Matt. 5.16; Matt. 19.21, Luke 18.22.
6 Gal. 5.22–23.
7 See e.g. Luther, *Reformation Writings* 1.318–9. To support his claim that all Christians are equal as followers of Christ, Luther appealed to a number of passages in the New Testament in which Christians are described collectively as a priesthood, e.g. 1 Pet. 1.3, 2.5–9; cf. Heb. 13.15–16; Rev. 1.6. Contemporaries and followers elaborated the argument: all Christians are sons of God (1 Pet. 1.3, 23; Gal. 3.26), kings, priests and prophets (1 Pet. 2.9). All receive the same Spirit, though it works in them in different ways (Rom. 12.6; 1 Cor. 12.4–11; Eph. 4.7).
8 *Methodist Principles of Church Order*, pp. 5–6.
9 According to Acts, Paul was much more zealously religious than any of the disciples is described as being (e.g. Acts 8.1–3, 9.1), and in his speech to the Sanhedrin (Acts 23.6), he describes himself as 'a Pharisee, a son of Pharisees'.
10 Rom. 12.4–8; 1 Cor. 12.4.

1 The meanings of love

1 C. S. Lewis uses these words for four different kinds of love in *The Four Loves*, but his use of them is some way from their meanings in Greek.
2 The Hebrew Bible was translated into Greek in Alexandria, in Egypt, in the third century BC. It was used by Greek-speaking Jews throughout the Mediterranean, including many of the first Christian converts, and it became the earliest version of the Old Testament used by Christians.

3 My translation. Anyone who is familiar with the Authorized Version of the Bible will notice that in this passage, it is closer to the Greek than many modern translations, because it sticks mostly to verbs: 'Charity suffereth long, and is kind; charity envieth not; charity vaunteth not itself . . .' Note that by 'Charity suffereth long' this version does not mean that charity suffers in a modern sense, but that love is longsuffering.

4 John Donne, *Devotions upon Emergent Occasions* (1624), 'Meditation XVII'.

5 'The spiritual power of matter', from Teilhard de Chardin, *Hymn of the Universe*, English edn (London, Collins, 1961), p. 62 (italics in original).

6 Mark 10.45 = Matt. 20.28.

7 There are many theories of salvation or atonement; see the 'Further resources' section at the end of this book for some books which give helpful summaries of the traditional theories or explore how salvation may be understood in the modern world.

8 I am grateful to Gavin McCormick for this observation.

2 Attentiveness: the ministry of listening

1 Rom. 12.1–8; 1 Cor. 12.1–26.

2 Neil Belton, *The Good Listener. Helen Bamber: A Life Against Cruelty* (London, Weidenfeld and Nicholson, 1998), p. 109.

3 Anne Long, *Listening* (London: Darton, Longman and Todd, 1990), p. 45.

4 Bill Kirkpatrick, *The Creativity of Listening* (London: Darton, Longman and Todd, 2005), pp. xiv–v.

3 The call to prophecy

1 Quoted in their Memoir of Elizabeth Fry (1780–1845), Quaker and Prison Reformer, by her daughters Katherine Fry and Rachel Cresswell (1847).

2 'The inhumanity of slavery', from Frederick Douglass, *My Bondage and My Freedom*, ed. J. D. Smith (New York: Random House, 2003), pp. 334–5.

3 Sheila Cassidy, *Sharing the Darkness: The Spirituality of Caring* (London, Darton, Longman and Todd, 1988), pp. 10–12.

4 Thomas Traherne, *Centuries of Meditations: First Century*, Ch. 12.

5 S. McFague, *The Body of God: An Ecological Theology* (Norwich: SCM Press, 1993), pp. 16–22, 142–4.

4 Forgiveness and reconciliation

1 Mark 9.14–29. The Greek verb here is *pisteuein*, the standard verb for 'believe', 'trust', 'have faith' or 'have confidence'.

2 Though this sentence does not appear in all manuscripts.

3 Tertullian, *On Prayer* 8; Cyprian, *On Prayer* 23. Both these, with Origen's *On Prayer*, are translated and introduced by Alistair Stewart-Sykes in *Tertullian, Cyprian, Origen, On the Lord's Prayer* (New York: St Vladimir's Seminary Press, 2004).

4 Origen, *On Prayer* 28.1–8.

5 John Allen, *Rabble-Rouser for Peace: The Authorized Biography of Desmond Tutu* (London: Rider, 2006), p. 347. Tutu's understanding of forgiveness is that it is available in God but not given until we ask for it.

5 Freeing the Spirit

1 Ed. and trans. H. Musurillo in *The Martyrs of Lyons* (Oxford, Clarendon, 1972), p. 69.

2 Musurillo, *Martyrs of Lyons*, p. 67.

3 London: Rider, 2001.

4 Anand: Gujarat Sahitya Prakash, 2005.

6 Living prayer

1 Luis of Granada, *Of Prayer and Meditation* (Paris, 1582) prol. 3.

2 Trans. Helen Waddell in *The Lives of the Desert Fathers* (London, Constable, 1936), p. 160.

3 Abhishiktananda *Prayer* (London, SPCK, 1972), pp. 1–2, 6.

4 Extracts from *The Way of a Pilgrim* (Anonymous, nineteenth(?)-century Russian), trans. Olga Savin (Boston, MA: Shambhala, 2001), pp. 8, 11–12.

5 *The Journal of George Fox*, rev. edn by John L. Nickalls (Philadelphia: Religious Society of Friends, 1997), pp. 4, 9–10.

7 Speaking of faith

1 In Chapter 17 of his rule, St Francis said that not all his brothers would be able to preach formally, but that they could and should all preach by their actions.

2 Chapters 20, 21, trans. A. Roberts and J. Donaldson (Edinburgh, 1885).

3 Tertullian, *Against Praxeas* 8.

4 Quoted in J.-J. Pérennès, *A Life Poured Out: Pierre Claverie of Algeria* (New York: Orbis Books, 2007), pp. 103–4.

5 From 'The third part of the sermon of salvation', one of the 'Homilies appointed to be read in churches', first published in 1547 and republished periodically with additions until 1623. Through these sermons, Cranmer and his fellow reformers aimed to educate the ordinary people in doctrine, prayer, morality and the practicalities of maintaining their churches. They were preached regularly in churches until the nineteenth century.

6 Christians, of course, also disagree among themselves about how it is appropriate to believe in certain traditions. Some, for instance, believe that miracles, the physical resurrection or the virgin birth are historical facts, while others regard these as myths which express something about the nature of God and salvation.

7 See Ch. 4 on whether we must forgive each other before we can be forgiven.

8 K. Koyama, *Waterbuffalo Theology* (London: Orbis Books, 1974), pp. vii–viii.

9 V. J. Donovan, *Christianity Rediscovered* (Maryknoll, NY: Orbis Books, 2003), p. 30.

10 Quoted in John Allen, *Rabble-Rouser for Peace: The Authorised Biography of Desmand Tutu* (New York: HarperOne, 2007), pp. 129–30.

11 Quoted in Allen, *Rabble-Rouser for Peace*, pp. 138–9.

12 D. O'Murchu, *Quantum Theology: Spiritual Implications of the New Physics*, rev. edn (New York: Crossroads, 2004), especially pp. 56–7.

13 Num. 11.12; Isa. 49.14–15 (suckling); Isa. 66.12–13 (comforting).

14 e.g. Deut. 32.11–12; Ps. 17.8, 36.7; Matt. 23.37.

15 M. Katoppo, *Compassionate and Free* (Geneva: World Council of Churches, 1979), pp. 65–6.

Further resources

CHRISM is the British society for Christians (lay and ordained) in secular ministry. Its mission is 'To help ourselves and others to celebrate the presence of God and the holiness of life in our work, and to see and tell the Christian story there.' Chrism holds retreats and an annual conference, publishes a newsletter and occasional papers, and is in regular touch with the European Worker Priest movement and the Tentmaking Association of America. Its website is at <www.chrism.org.uk> and information can also be obtained from the Membership Secretary (contact details on the website).

A number of bodies train volunteers in the basics of counselling; there are also many courses for professional counsellors. CRUSE trains people to work with the bereaved of all ages and situations. It has a website and publicity materials which can be obtained from public libraries and Citizens' Advice Bureaux. The Open College runs distance-learning courses. The Institute of Counselling advertises both distance learning and college-based courses. Both have helpful websites, as do <www.mediatortraining.org.uk> and *The Guardian* website <www.guardian.co.uk>, which list courses nationwide.

All the authors and works cited in the text are well worth reading. Below are a few more suggestions:

Religion in everyday life

Ronald Blythe, *Word from Wormingford* (Norwich: Canterbury Press, 1997).
Teilhard de Chardin, *Hymn of the Universe* (London: Collins, 1965).
Quaker Faith and Practice (London: The Religious Society of Friends, 1995 edition).
The Rule of St Benedict, trans. J. McCann (London: Sheed and Ward, 1972).
Edith Stein, *Essential Writings*, selected with an introduction by J. Sullivan OCD (New York: Orbis Books, 2002).
W. H. Vanstone, *Love's Endeavour, Love's Expense* (London: Darton, Longman and Todd, 1977).

W. H. Vanstone, *The Stature of Waiting* (London: Darton, Longman and Todd, 1982).

The Way of a Pilgrim and The Pilgrim Continues His Way, trans. O. Savin (Boston, MA: Shambhala, 2001).

Theology of work etc.

P. Ballard and J. Pritchard, *Practical Theology in Action*, 2nd edn (London: SPCK, 2006).

David Clark, *Breaking the Mould of Christendom: Kingdom Community, Diaconal Church and the Liberation of the Laity* (Peterborough: Epworth Press, 2005).

Margaret Joachim, 'M Without the SE?', *Ministers-at-Work, The Journal for Christians in Secular Ministry* 102 (July 2007), 17–21.

Edward Lucas, 'Service, Solidarity and Self: A Christian Ethic in a Competitive Workplace', reprinted in *Ministers-at-Work, The Journal for Christians in Secular Ministry* 94 (July 2005), 7–23.

J. Mantle, *Britain's First Worker Priests: Radical Ministry in a Post-war Setting* (Norwich: SCM Press, 2000).

Henri Perrin, *Priest and Worker: The Autobiography of Henri Perrin* (London: Macmillan, 1965).

Thinking about the meaning of being Christian

John Barton, *Living Belief: Being Christian – Being Human* (London: Continuum, 2005).

Christian Believing: The Nature of Christian Faith and its Expression in Holy Scripture and Creeds (London: Doctrine Commission of the Church of England, 1976).

John Pritchard, *How to Explain Your Faith* (London: SPCK, 2006).

Timothy Radcliffe OP, *What is the Point of Being a Christian?* (London: Continuum, 2005).

Gerd Theissen, *The First Followers of Jesus*, trans. J. Bowden (Norwich: SCM Press, 1978).

Keith Ward, *God: A Guide for the Perplexed* (Oxford: Oneworld, 2002).

Maurice Wiles, *Reason to Believe* (Norwich: SCM Press, 1999).

H. A. Williams, *The True Wilderness* (Harmondsworth: Penguin, 1968).

Contemplative prayer

Abhishiktananda, *Prayer* (London: SPCK, 1972).

Anon., *The Cloud of Unknowing*, ed. and trans. William Johnston (London: Fount, 1997).

Augustin Guillerand, *Where Silence is Praise: From the Writings of Dom Augustin Guillerand O.Cart* (London: Darton, Longman and Todd, 1960).

Andrew Louth, *The Wilderness of God* (London: Darton, Longman and Todd, 2003).

John Main, *Word into Silence* (London: Darton, Longman and Todd, 1980).

Thomas Merton, *Elected Silence* (London: Hollis and Carter, 1949).

Helpful material from other faith traditions

Thich Nhat Hanh, *The Blooming of a Lotus: Guided Meditation for Achieving the Miracle of Mindfulness* (Boston, MA: Beacon Press, 1993).

Lao Tzu, *Tao Te Ching: A Book about the Way and the Power of the Way*, a new version by Ursula K. le Guin (Boston, MA: Shambhala, 1998).